Love Your Home Again

ANN LIGHTFOOT & KATE PAWLOWSKI

Love Your Home Again

ORGANIZE YOUR SPACE AND UNCOVER
THE HOME OF YOUR DREAMS

Library of Congress Cataloging-in-Publication Data available.

ISBN 978-1-7972-1687-4

Manufactured in China.

Photography by Julia D'Agostino.

Design and typesetting by Kelley Galbreath. Typeset in Freight and Verlag.

10 9 8 7 6 5 4 3 2 1

Chronicle books and gifts are available at special quantity discounts to corporations, professional associations, literacy programs, and other organizations. For details and discount information, please contact our premiums department at corporatesales@chroniclebooks.com or at 1-800-759-0190.

CHRONICLE PRISM

Chronicle Prism is an imprint of Chronicle Books LLC
680 Second Street, San Francisco, California 94107

www.chronicleprism.com

To our clients,

For the last decade, you've trusted us with your homes and allowed us into your lives. So many of you have become friends. Without you, Done & Done Home would not exist and for that we are eternally grateful.

Contents

Introduction

Get ready to love your home again

TEN YEARS AGO, WHEN WE STARTED DONE & DONE HOME, a professional organizing and move management business, we had no idea what the future held. We only knew that we were happiest working together and being in the service of others. They were long days of hard, physical work and we found that the ability to leave our clients' homes better than we found them a day or two earlier was deeply satisfying. Eventually what had been an unformed thought—a feeling, maybe—became the ethos for our company. We believe when you enter the outside world from a home full of ease, beauty, laughter, and hope, the energy of the world changes for the better; and that change can be achieved through efficient systems of household management. We've worked hard to make this a reality for thousands of people.

In a time where photo-ready homes are always front and center online and in magazines, the discrepancy between people's expectations of their own homes and the reality of them can cause a ton of stress. They may realize that inefficiency, disorganization, and lack of household systems in their homes are part of the problem, but they have no idea how to fix that. They love how soothing and glamorous the Insta-worthy pantries and closets are and they want some of that for themselves, though they know they'd probably be just as content if they could find everybody's shoes with ease and get out the door on time.

We believe in organizing not just for organizing's sake. Creating and implementing systems that keep a home running smoothly is essential for everyone, especially parents, so they have time to do things that are more fulfilling, such as spending time with families, exercising, sleeping, cooking, playing, and reading. You'll see the headers for each section include some of the goals for each space.

After nearly a decade of digging people out of domestic disasters, we have acquired a vast knowledge of how to implement systems to make our clients' homes function well, and in turn, make their lives function better.

When people first move into their homes, they have clear ideas about what they want from every room. The bedrooms will be peaceful and cozy. The dining room will work well for entertaining friends and family. The kitchen will be a hub of activity, but it will also be high-functioning and easy to manage. Then time passes and clutter happens. Drawers, closets, and cabinets get loaded with stuff, making it difficult to put things away. Everyday tasks take over free time, and the joy of spending time at home diminishes.

In *Love Your Home Again*, we'll teach you how to manage your home in a way that is modern, kind, effective, and fair. Though some people's problems are decades in the making, we'll show you that no home is beyond help. No one wants to spend all their free time doing chores—and through our systems of decluttering, organizing, and maintaining, you won't have to.

We'll guide you through the steps needed to resolve the issues behind the excess, teach you how to clear the unneeded objects out of your home, and set you up to go forward with a plan to acquire any new belongings you may want or need in a thoughtful, eco-friendly way. We will show you how to revise the dreams you had for your home before you moved in to include the knowledge of who you are today and how you and your family actually live in your home. For example, the dining room is great for entertaining but, with enough storage and a system for tidying up, it can be modified to use as a homework room or a home office as well.

We'll make it fun. We'll make it clear. We can't wait for you to rediscover the home of your dreams.

Prepare for Success

Key concepts and tips for
getting started

TERMS WE USE

- **OWNING WELL**—Everything we will teach you supports our philosophy of Owning Well. When we use this term, we mean buying the best quality you can afford, which we call an "Intentional Investment," and learning to take care of your things so that they last, which we call "Mindful Maintenance." Yes, you may spend more on individual items—but ultimately you will have less of everything, and what you do have will work better and last longer. It's not only for the sake of your home but for the sake of the planet as well.

- **IT GETS WORSE BEFORE IT GETS BETTER**—This is always true when you're decluttering properly, because you will need to pull everything out of its home for proper sorting. Your house will look like a bomb went off in whatever room you're working in that day. That's OK! Just stay with it, and never move on to another room until the first one is finished, with all items put away and the room returned to working order.

- **SUNK COST**—This refers to money that has already been spent and cannot be recovered.

The money was spent when you purchased the item, and holding on to it doesn't make it more valuable to you. All of the extra items in our homes are there because we purchased items we don't necessarily need, and then later we fear getting rid of them in case we'll need them in the future. The truth is, people tend to err on the side of caution and hold on to too much. Push yourself hard to be realistic. In the kitchen, for example, people rarely get rid of things they later want. If you're nervous about this, realize that a cake pan can be borrowed for a single use, or you could improvise with a pan you already own.

- **HOLDER-ON-ER**—We call people who have a strong aversion to letting go of things "Holder-on-ers" because "hoarders" sounds harsh and makes us think of people who need medical professionals to treat an underlying mental health condition. When people tell us they're hoarders or they have a family member who is a hoarder, they usually don't intend it as a "diagnosis" but say it because they are frustrated with how they or their relative is living among too much clutter. If we are able to help, that usually

means there's simply a tendency to hold on to more things than can reasonably fit in the living space. If it's completely out of control and we can't help, that might mean there is a condition that needs a mental health expert to resolve. If it's a matter of breaking deeply ingrained habits, we can often make a big difference—and so can you.

- **SAVE FOREVER**—This is the term we use for personal memorabilia that you want to keep. These things don't have actual use, but they are a map of where you've been and often remind you of the people and places that matter to you. The most important thing is to curate this collection periodically and store it in proper bins, so it doesn't get ruined.

BEST STRATEGIES

- **TAKE *EVERY SINGLE THING* OUT FROM WHERE IT LIVES**—Things have a tendency to stay in the space they're in even if you don't really need, use, or even like them. That's just the way it is. Remember Newton's first law of motion? *A body at rest stays at rest unless acted*

upon by an unbalanced force. The unbalancing force will have to be you. That closet full of odd items and those drawers full of stray belongings will stay at rest for years unless you unbalance them. If you want those drawers and closets to run efficiently, you'll need to empty them completely so you can see clearly what's there and find better homes for the items that need to move.

- **KEEP LIKE WITH LIKE**—Always store similar items together. Separating your belongings into categories and subcategories immediately shows us where the clutter is. For instance, gather all of your sweaters into one area and divide them into subcategories by fabric or style. If you own ten striped cotton sweaters but only wear five, that would be a great place to edit. A very large stack of jeans doesn't seem so bad, but when you subdivide by color—dark, light, black, gray, and white—and then by leg width and length, you'll quickly decide if the dark skinny jeans are still your style . . . or if they're ready for giving away.

- **WATCH THE FRONT DOOR**—This is the expression that we use to keep ourselves and our clients from buying and buying and buying. Put the brakes on whenever and wherever you can, and you'll find your home is much easier to handle in the future. When you're shopping online or in an actual store, even the grocery store, slow down and ask yourself if you'll use everything you're about to purchase once it's inside your front door. Maybe try and take a couple of things out of your cart (or "cart") just to see how easy it is *not* to buy something.

- **LIVE BY THE 10 PERCENT REDUCTION RULE**—If any area in your home feels tight, it likely means there's too much stuff. People get overwhelmed by the thought of having to purge everything they own and live like minimalists. That's not necessary! If you can reduce any category by 10 percent you will notice a huge difference. It will be easier to find what you are looking for and easier to put things away.

- **DONATE WISELY**—We all hate to waste, but some items can't be donated and need to be thrown away. Before you go to the effort of packing up items for donating, consider what will be of real use to someone else. While we don't want to fill the landfills, we also don't want to burden the staff at donation centers. It's worth a call to your local Goodwill or other charitable organization to find out if they want stained or torn clothes or linens for textile recycling, or if

they only want things that individuals will use in their current state.

- **DECIDE LATER**—While sorting, don't slow down for deep thinking. There will be items that are clearly meant for keeping and those that are meant for giving away. There will also be items that make you say things like "Hmm, I don't know . . ." or, "I mean, I still like it . . ." or, "It was so expensive that I can't just get rid of it, but I don't really use it." Don't do any of this hemming and hawing in the moment of decluttering. Instead,

put those "I don't know" items right into the "to be decided" pile. You'll come back to them! All will be revealed in the fullness of time.

- **OTHER PEOPLE'S BELONGINGS**—Before you get rid of anything that belongs to another family member, consult them. Getting rid of other people's things can cause problems that get bigger over time. We've had many clients whose family members have thrown things away without asking, and years later the clients still feel anxious about decluttering and therefore resist the process.

- **PATIENCE WITH OTHERS AND COMPASSION FOR YOURSELF**—These are the best strategies for decluttering your home. If this were

easy, your home and everybody else's would function perfectly.

SUPPLIES WE RECOMMEND HAVING ON HAND

- **BLACK GARBAGE BAGS FOR ACTUAL GARBAGE**—We love heavy-duty garbage bags ("contractor bags") because they never rip

and hold more than a standard kitchen bag. Be careful not to overfill them, making them too heavy to lift. We made that mistake often in the beginning and it makes the whole process more exhausting than it needs to be.

- **CLEAR GARBAGE BAGS AND OTHER ITEMS FOR RECYCLING AND DONATING**—We use clear contractor bags on all of our

organizing jobs for the same reasons we use black contractor bags, but we use clear ones so that the donation items and/or recycling items don't just get thrown in the garbage.

- **SHOPPING BAGS AND TOTE BAGS**—We use the ones that clients are getting rid of for donating, so make sure to keep potentially useful ones until the process is finished. You'll avoid using more plastic bags than necessary.

- **EMPTY BOXES**—If you have boxes that you've been saving out in the garage, now is the time to use them. Kitchen items for donating may be better off in a box so they don't break or chip. Old newspapers or paper bags that will be going out anyway can be used to pack up breakables.

- **STICKY NOTES**—These are great for labeling items you have divided into sections (such as Donate, Trash, Keep, Repair) while you're sorting and for generally keeping notes about the process.

- **LABEL MAKER**—This is not a requirement, but it really does make organizing easier, and one roll of tape goes a very long way. If you do choose to use one, we've found that if you only tear off half of the backing (it's already divided) it will stick fine but is easier to remove.

- **TAPE MEASURE**—This will come in handy if you are going to buy new bins, baskets, drawer dividers, shelving units—it will

ensure the items you buy fit properly in the spaces they're intended to fill.

- **BOX CUTTER**—This is great for opening up all those stored-away boxes as well as breaking down boxes for recycling.

For links to our favorite products and additional resources, visit us at www.doneanddonehome.com/resources.

Kitchen

A stress-free environment for nurturing and nourishing yourself and your family

WE WANT YOU TO HAVE AN ORGANIZED KITCHEN—not just because it looks good but because it will inspire you and everyone else who uses your kitchen to enjoy the process of food preparation and reduce the stress that often surrounds this everyday chore.

The kitchen is the busiest room in the home, and it is one of the areas that people struggle with the most. Everything from unloading the dishwasher to getting breakfast on the table can be difficult if your kitchen is inefficient. We all would prefer our mornings to be joyful and stress-free. Everyone envisions being kind to the people they live with and leaving them on a high note each day but, in reality, mornings can be hard on everyone. Worst of all, if the kitchen chaos is just one part of an entire house that doesn't function well, no matter how hard you try you will inevitably snap at someone. And if that someone is a young person, you will feel bad about it all day.

It doesn't have to be like that. A high-functioning kitchen reduces stress and supports:

- **CONNECTION AND COMMUNITY** by making it easier to share meals with family and friends
- **HEALTHY CHOICES** with meal planning and cooking
- **BETTER FINANCES** because less food is wasted

Most people don't think to declutter or reorganize their kitchens unless it happens during a move—almost incidentally. They know the kitchen isn't working for them, but they assume it's the fault of the actual kitchen—its size, layout, or both. Generally, it's not. It's the fault of all the extra stuff. It's imperative to clear the space with intention because you want this workhorse of a room to support the life you are trying to live.

How Do You Use Your Kitchen?

Before you begin to organize your kitchen, consider how you (and any people you share your home with) actually live. Expectations must meet reality—about who you are and about the space you live in. Be realistic as you answer these questions:

- **HOW OFTEN DO YOU COOK?** Are you cooking from scratch— or heating a few things up?
- **IF YOU HAVE CHILDREN AT HOME, HOW OLD ARE THEY?**
- **DO YOU ENTERTAIN?** How often?
- **WHEN WAS THE LAST TIME** you tried to get something out of that cabinet you can't reach?
- **WOULD YOU LIKE TO COOK/BAKE/ENTERTAIN MORE** than you currently do, but it's too hard?

Our clients often ask us if we're horrified by how much stuff they have. We're not; not at all. Our role is not to judge. We're here to help you live as peacefully as possible in the space you have with the things you need, use, and want.

Whether you never, ever cook a thing or you have a sit-down family dinner every weeknight and dinner parties on the weekend, what we care about is organizing your kitchen so that the items you use on a daily or

What
do you do
in here
anyway?

weekly basis are readily available. We care that when you do entertain, you
can easily find what you're looking for and that you enjoy the process of
welcoming friends and family into your home. We care that cleaning up is
a breeze so you'll never dread it.

Your kitchen has bigger problems than these lovely dishes.

SORT AND DECIDE

This is where we tell our clients, "It gets worse before it gets better." Partway through this process it may look like you've trashed your own home, but we promise the end result is worth it.

1 To begin, **PULL OUT EVERYTHING** from the cabinets and drawers, one category at a time. We suggest starting with items that are larger and thus less likely to have been purchased without thought, like pots and pans.

2 Now, **SORT** the items into subcategories by type and size. For example, nonstick frying pans are one subcategory and cast-iron pans are another.

3 Next, **SET ASIDE** the items you never use, no matter what they cost. Sometimes cookware comes in sets and while one or two of the pans become favorites, the others still look brand-new. Unused lids take up precious space, so definitely let those go. Objects in good condition can often be donated; the rest can be thrown away.

4 Now, **EXAMINE** the items you do use. Are they still working well for you? If the coating from a nonstick pan is chipped or worn away, make a note of the size of the pan and add it to your to-buy list. It's worn out because you always choose it—but no need to keep a pan that is potentially dangerous to your health. The worn-out, sticky, chipped ones can go to garbage or recycling, while the perfectly good ones that aren't useful to you can be donated.

5 **REVIEW WHAT'S LEFT.** You will likely end up with a few you are unsure about. Put those in a to-be-decided pile. At the very end of the kitchen declutter, look at this pile and put back anything you might use in the future and, if it can easily fit, keep it. No need to potentially buy it again.

 These are the basics of decluttering. This system can be applied to all areas of the kitchen and to the rest of your home.

THE ITEMS THAT MYSTERIOUSLY MULTIPLY

You might think everyday dishes, glasses, and silverware are a big part of the problem in your kitchen, but that is rarely the case. The biggest problems in the kitchen occur in these categories where things magically multiply:

- Mugs
- Tupperware
- Cooking utensils
- Water bottles
- Children's plastic dishes
- "Great" saved jars
- Florist vases

Multiplication happens most often with smaller, less-expensive items. Rarely does someone buy a stand mixer on a whim—but wooden spoons and spatulas? Oh, yes. We're never in a kitchen where the homeowner says, "Oh, wow. I didn't realize I had three stand mixers. Where'd those come from?" But when we pull out all the utensils, the homeowner is often stunned.

Seldom does anyone have a lot of random plates and glasses. Even if they're missing a few plates and some glasses have broken and been replaced with others that don't match, usually all those things fit in the cabinets they've been assigned to. The problem is that every extra inch is taken up with those ten water bottles. The Tupperware—both the good ones and the plastic delivery containers that were "too good to throw out"—have expanded to all the extra drawer and cabinet space. The kids may be in high school now but the sippy cups and beloved TV character plates still hold a place of honor. And those mugs that started out on one shelf and have grown to cover two or three—who is using all of those?

Let's break it down.

Mugs

Get rid of the mugs you never really liked. You know the ones—the one with the handle that's too small and too low down on the cup, the one that's too thick, the one that's so wide your coffee cools off in a minute. Three mugs for each adult in your home should be more than enough for everyday life. You can keep extras for entertaining up on a higher shelf. Impossible to part with some of them for sentimental reasons? Move them to the top, hard-to-reach shelf so they still catch your eye every now and again.

Tupperware

Pull out all that Tupperware and its ugly cousin, delivery containers. Match up all the bottoms with the tops and get rid of anything that isn't a set. If you are not able to recycle Tupperware where you live, that is unfortunate, but you have to throw it away sooner or later, so throw it away now—and when your plastic containers are organized you may be able to

Ugly mugs and warped containers be gone!

TUPPERWARE

stop buying more. Now take a hard look at what's left. This is where reality versus fantasy comes into play. Do you have forty sets but are certain to order in again next week? Do you need that many because you cook so much that you freeze some or send your grown kids back to their apartments with food? **It doesn't matter how much you have—it matters how much you actually use.** Create the space for it and hold yourself to that space.

We have a client who keeps her Tupperware contained in a large plastic storage bin under her kitchen sink. She likes the limitation it imposes because she tends to hold on to more than she needs.

More isn't better with spoons.

Utensils

Spatulas and wooden spoons are always categories of clutter. Somehow, we choose our favorite of these each time we need one and move on to lesser favorites if the best one is dirty or in use. *Envision your toughest cooking/baking scenario:* What's the maximum amount you'd use at any one time? There is a number that makes sense for each kitchen. Sometimes for spatulas that's three or four; you can decide the number that's right for you, but it's very rarely twelve. In a small apartment, the right numbers could be two spatulas and three wooden or silicone spoons.

Pantry

Empty your food cabinets and your pantry. Take every single thing out and put it on the counters or the kitchen table. Group it like-with-like and then place it in subcategories; so grains are all in one area and then rice, quinoa, couscous, etc., are each in their own group. Do the same with canned food, snacks, spices, and baking goods.

Once everything is out of hiding, go back in and give your storage space a good cleaning. You will be surprised how dirty pantries and cupboards can get. We generally don't use shelf liners because they're time consuming to install and don't seem to help enough with the cleaning process to make it worthwhile. If we're worried about things that will potentially drip, like oil, we put those on a lazy Susan that can easily be removed and washed.

Within each category, check expiration dates and throw away anything past the date. Yes, we know that sell-by dates are a guide, and the food may still be good, but we also know that you didn't eat it for years so you're unlikely to eat it now. The uneaten canned peas that remind you of your grandfather will remain unused, so no need to keep them in your home.

Refrigerator

If you have a bunch of containers filling up your fridge from weeks past, your new food will get mixed up and pushed around and ultimately wasted. Take everything out of your fridge. Wipe down the shelves and drawers and only put back the food that is truly going to be eaten. Don't hold on to bottles of trendy ingredients or unusual sauces you used once and never returned to. Eventually, it will have to be thrown away. Go ahead and be ruthless now to make space for new choices going forward.

Trust us, clean out your fridge!

Freezer

Freezers tend to be dumping grounds. Hanging on to food because you feel wasteful tossing it is a decision deferred. Like everywhere else in your home, we recommend removing everything from the freezer. We would say everything but the ice cubes, but even ice can be a problem. Remember those silicone molds your husband used for the large ice cubes that year he was into bourbon? Those are still in there, just way in the back. And the automatic ice maker bin? The bottom layer has been there for ages so why not freshen up the whole freezer while you're clearing it out? Dump the ice and put everything else on the counter and give yourself a moment to think it through. Mysterious frozen packages? Items that are freezer burned? Healthy breakfast muffins from when you froze an extra batch when your kid liked healthy breakfast muffins? Was that already a year ago? Throw it all away and start fresh.

Alcohol

People often keep alcohol—both wine and spirits—in the kitchen. This may be related to the fact that people don't usually have bars in their homes like they once did, or it may be because of the disappearing dining room where a bar cart could be stored. In any event, entertaining supplies take up a lot of space in the kitchen. It's another category that tends to collect a lot of unused items, some that were gifts and some that just stay around long after anyone drank an appletini. Yes, someone may want an Aperol spritz or a cosmopolitan at your next party. But you simply can't plan for every possible thing that someone, sometime may want. Your daily life shouldn't be cluttered up in preparation for Uncle Frank's once-a-year Brandy Alexander. Your guests will happily have a glass of white wine or a craft beer—and when they're dying for a fancy cocktail they'll go to that new bar in town, and perhaps invite you along to repay you for dinner.

Spices

It can take a long time to use spices that aren't in the "big ten"—thyme, rosemary, cinnamon, paprika, oregano, garlic powder, onion powder, chili powder, bay leaves, and now turmeric, since it's supposed to be so good for you.

In November and December, you may get through some cloves, cardamom, ginger, and nutmeg—but we realized recently that most people don't get through one of those spice jars of whole nutmeg in a decade. Seriously, you grate and grate that thing and you have a quarter of a teaspoon, which is all you need for your annual pumpkin pie, and then you put it back in the jar till next year.

Like every area of your home and every decision you make on what stays and what goes, you have to be honest about what's happening here. Do you have spices that are more than five years old? You wouldn't be

This is how your spice drawer could look!

alone. We all pick up spices mindlessly at the grocery store when we decide to make chili but can't remember if we have any cumin at home.

To clean up your spice game, **pull them all out**. Get rid of any duplicates. If you didn't write a date on the bottom with a Sharpie when you bought it, open and smell each one and keep the one that's stronger. Also get rid of any that you don't use. When we were clearing out our own spices recently, we had to google "marjoram" to find out what it's used for because we each had a full bottle. It turns out its most common uses are in soap and English roast goose with chestnut stuffing. We tossed ours.

Now that you've narrowed down forty spice jars to twenty, take one more pass at it. Can anything else go? I know the same old song is playing in your head—"I'll just have to rebuy it if I throw it out now," with a chorus of "It cost good money"—but if you aren't using it currently and haven't in years, then you *should* rebuy it when you need it. And if you don't use it often, next time buy the small jar. It isn't as pretty on the shelf, but it cuts down on waste. Professional chefs use up their spices every six months and recommend home cooks don't keep theirs for more than a year. They don't go bad, but they do lose their potency. And whole spices like nutmeg? Those should be replaced every two to four years.

Tea

Get real—how much tea do you actually drink? Grocery stores and tea companies are marketing gurus, and they fill us with notions of coziness, hope, strength, friendship, health, and calm—and we're all buying it! All of us. Americans spend over $10 billion a year on tea. We've thrown away so many boxes of tea in the last ten years in our clients' homes and yes, even in our own homes. As careful as we try to be, that Sleepytime bear in the stocking cap napping on the fluffy couch has also given us hope of rest.

Ask yourself the usual questions and be firm with yourself:

- **DO YOU REALLY DRINK TEA** and, if so, how often?
- **IF YOUR ANSWER IS ONCE OR TWICE A WEEK,** and only in the winter, it'll take many cold winters to get through twelve boxes of tea.
- **HOW LONG HAS IT BEEN IN THERE—YEARS?** That wouldn't be unusual, but tea is at its best if consumed within three to four months if it came in a bag/box and up to a year in a tin.

Here's a reasonable amount of tea. How much do you have?

We recommend keeping only what you actually drink and a selection to offer guests (if in fact you ever offer anyone a cup of tea). We each have a plastic tea bag storage container and fill the sections with a sampling of green tea, herbal tea, a decaf black tea, and a regular black tea.

Small Appliances

If your prime cabinet space is clogged with a rice cooker or specialty coffee maker because "Maybe someday" or "It was a gift" or "I spent $50 on it," to that we say, "So what?" Honestly, you did your part when you thanked your college roommate, Cheryl, for the panini press she got you for a wedding present. She didn't expect you to marry it. You've used it twice in ten years

Storing Small Appliances

BECCA, WHO LOVES TO COOK, had so many appliances all over the kitchen and basement that we grouped them together and worked with her to decide what was staying and what was going. She got rid of all sorts of appliances she no longer used and picked the best of things like popcorn poppers, coffee grinders, and countertop grills. We then cleared a floor-to-ceiling cabinet that had been holding items that could be housed elsewhere, and put all the small appliances together. And there, "appliance city" was born! We now use this term with all our clients for any area where we store appliances together. The only thing that makes Becca different from anyone else is that she had the space to store her many appliances in one large cabinet. Most of us are limited on space, but even if it's a smaller area, consider creating your own "appliance city," so you know exactly what you have.

so let it go. Cheryl is also trying to create more space in her kitchen without moving or doing an expensive renovation. Cheryl understands.

One of the reasons there are so many appliances in every kitchen is that they're expensive and therefore most people are hesitant to get rid of them. Also, many of them tie into some pretty basic fantasies of home:

- **BAKING CAKES** with the kids? You'll need a stand mixer for sure!
- **BREAKFAST IN BED** on father's day? A waffle maker should do the trick!
- **MAKING SMOOTHIES** for fitness and weight loss? We'll definitely need a Vitamix!
- **QUICK-COOKING RICE** and hard-boiled eggs that are easy to peel? Let's get an Instant Pot!

Oh, the life you'll be living!

That was the fantasy. Now, it's time for reality. Are you really using the appliances you've collected? Let's find out. First, pull out all your appliances, then sort them, like-with-like, placing items into subcategories like coffee-making devices.

Now, get real with yourself and ask, "When did I last use this?" or even, "When was the last time *anyone* used this?" Do the math: If you haven't used the Keurig in four years and you drink three cups a day, that would be 3 cups x 365 days a year x 4 years = 4,380 times you didn't choose to use the Keurig. Guess what? You aren't going to choose it now, or anytime soon. It's time for it to go.

Keep Your Kitchen Running Smoothly

Once you've chosen what's going to stay, look around the kitchen to determine the best possible spot for each item based on how often you will use it in the future. Choose wisely where things go, with these strategies in mind:

Easy To Lift

Easy to reach

Easy to find

Easy to grab

- **YOUR MOST FREQUENTLY USED** dishes, glasses, and silverware: Store these as close to the dishwasher as possible.

- **HEAVY ITEMS,** like small appliances, belong in lower cabinets that are easier to reach.

- **INFREQUENTLY USED ITEMS** can be stored in deep, less convenient cabinets.

- **GOT YOUNG KIDS?** Create a station near the dishwasher for kids' dishware. Systems that help your children become independent are good for everybody, and being able to grab their own dishes to set the table or unload the dishwasher are great places place to start.

- **MEANWHILE, OLDER KIDS WILL BE MORE LIKELY TO HELP** in the kitchen if they know where everything belongs. Your fourteen-year-old is less likely to complain about unloading the dishwasher if it doesn't require thinking, strategizing, or stacking coffee mugs where they don't fit easily.

- **WHO SAID ALL CLEANING SUPPLIES NEED TO LIVE UNDER THE SINK?** Keep your all-purpose cleaning spray under the sink, where it's easily accessible, along with dishwasher pods, dish liquid, and garbage bags. Move the rest out of this prime real estate and take advantage of all that room for things you use every week.

- **TRYING TO BE ECO-FRIENDLY?** Make sure you have a large supply of cloth napkins, dish towels, and rags at the ready. It's also a great idea to have a mini laundry bin under the sink to toss them in since they're often wet. You can put it in the space you freed up by moving the cleaning supplies!

- **WANT TO ENTERTAIN MORE?** Make sure your serving pieces are easily accessible—and not stacked in a cumbersome pile.

PANTRY ORGANIZATION

In recent years, gorgeous pantries have become all the rage, and while we love a giant pantry with storage bins and decanted foods, not everyone is able to achieve that (and maybe they don't want to). A high-functioning pantry does not need to look a certain way. It needs to be laid out so that it's easy for you and anyone you live with to find what they're looking for, and easy to put things back. This applies whether your pantry is a large walk-in closet or a cabinet and drawers where you keep the food. If you want to go for the matching bins and glass jars, have at it! But it's not a requirement.

PRO TIP:

Mix-and-Match Pasta

When you wind up with small amounts of various kinds of pasta, make a big batch of mixed pasta! Be sure to add them to your boiling water one by one, to account for various cooking times.

Pasta

Keep all pasta together in the pantry, possibly in a bin, but certainly in a designated area on the shelf. Pasta is purchased frequently and often goes unused. Don't let that happen. When it's all together in a bin, or is in one place, you can see what you have and use it up.

Grains

When did the explosion of exotic grains happen? People now have five kinds of rice, in addition to amaranth, quinoa, oats, millet, bulgur, and buckwheat. Be ruthless when sorting grains. We all buy them full of hope for the adventure and then they just sit there when we microwave a bag of rice. No judgment about having the hope, of course . . . but get real when you're organizing the millet.

Baking

Keep your baking items together. Whether this is the boxes of brownie and cake mix or every flour known to man, they should all be in the same area. For some of you, these items will be decanted on a shelf, and for others they could be in a bin on the floor of the pantry. In the baking bin you can also put sugars and cocoa, dry yeast, baking soda, and baking powder, etc.—in other words, all the things you're likely to pull out together when you get ready to use your stand mixer.

CHIPS

PASTA

GRAINS

SNACKS

SALTY   SWEET   SWEET

Chips and Snacks

Why can't snacks come in uniform boxes that we can see through? The chip bags don't stack or even line up easily and the boxes with two Ritz crackers take up so much space. Nobody wants a stale cracker or cookie when there's a new box to open and enjoy. We suggest decanting or putting all the bags together in a pantry storage bin.

Cereal

Like the chips and cookies, cereal stays fresher when it's decanted. The containers aren't cheap to begin with but once you notice how much less you're throwing away, and therefore buying, you'll be happy you made the investment.

Cans

Cans are to the pantry what board games are to the toy closet. People think they're going to use them "all the time" but never do. Yes, beans for chili. Yes, tomatoes. No, for sauerkraut, low-sodium soups, and last year's cranberry and pumpkin. Again (and again) there's fantasy involved

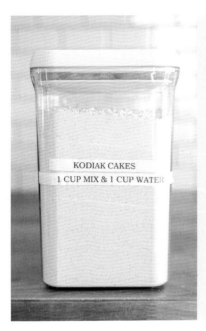

KODIAK CAKES
1 CUP MIX & 1 CUP WATER

PRO TIP:
Clear Containers

If you decant your chips, cookies, and other snacks into sealable containers, everything stays fresh longer and you can see what you have. This makes shopping easier, with the added bonus of less waste. Clear bins with a fun sealer button are much more likely to get resealed by your children than bags are with the chip clip. Crunchy items remain crunchy, so less waste and more money in the bank. OK, maybe only four or five dollars at a time—but it adds up. If you're worried about the expiration date, write it on the back of the container with a paint pen (easily removed with rubbing alcohol).

CANS

BAKING SUPPLIES

CEREAL

Junk drawer to functional drawer.

regarding what is picked up at the store. Donate unused items while they're still in-date and somebody else can use them.

Junk Drawer

Almost every home has one of these, and it is extremely useful. But you should clean it out frequently; make it a ten-minute job rather than an hour-long sorting extravaganza. We recommend a divided drawer insert (like the ones you use for silverware) to make sections for pens, extra keys, small tools, scissors, tape, twist ties, and rubber bands. Alternately, buy the small plastic drawer organizers from the Container Store that allow you to use every inch of space. If this is a combined place—junk drawer meets tiny office—you'll want to keep the sections distinct from one another.

MEAL PREP

Food prep is all the rage, and for good reason! Food prep recipes lay out how to prepare an entire week's worth of food, rather than a meal at a time. Being organized in the kitchen can save you time and money and even improve your health. Pinterest has a million and one food-prepping recipes (which we highly recommend checking out) for every diet imaginable, but we have some tips for making the actual process work for you.

Keep the Menu Simple

There's a time and a place to get adventurous in the kitchen. New recipes, trendy appliances, and unique produce can all be fun, but they can also be disastrous when it comes to prepping your meals for the week. That recipe may look amazing online, but if it's not a crowd-pleaser, you may be stuck with a huge hole in your lineup. Stick with the classics, and the week's meals will go smoothly. Save your grandmother's risotto for a day when you have ample time to enjoy the process.

Create Theme Nights

This may sound simplistic or too regimented for you, but hear us out. If you have a theme such as Meatless Mondays or Taco Tuesdays, you won't have to reinvent the wheel every single week. It gives you a jumping-off point for creativity. Meatless Monday could be anything from pasta to chili to vegetarian subs. Tacos could be vegetarian or filled with fish, beef, or chicken. Just because the theme is the same doesn't mean things will have to be boring—and working within a framework will keep you going week after week.

A Rotating Menu

SUSAN IS AN EXPERT on managing a kitchen. A mother of three kids under ten, she is an accomplished lawyer who spent a good amount of time implementing amazing systems in her home, so she doesn't have to think about them on a daily basis. One of her best is a three-week rotating grocery and dinner list. She says that her children don't notice that it is a rotating menu. She shops and does prep on Sundays and then doesn't have to spend any other time focusing on what to feed her family that week. Whether it's her husband, their nanny, or she herself who prepares it, dinner is a cinch.

Myth Busted

"Shopping in bulk always saves you money."

ALTHOUGH YOU CAN SAVE BY BUYING IN BULK at Costco and other big-box stores, if not handled properly this approach can cause stress and ultimately cost money. Things that don't go bad—paper towels, toilet paper, tissues, water, drinks, sometimes even snacks that seem to last forever—are great purchases so long as you can fit them in your home. We've been to New York City apartments where the paper towel packages are piled up in the living room and there are stacked rolls of toilet paper in the bathroom because they just don't fit anywhere else. Front hall closets might become dry-goods pantries just so all the bulk stuff has a place to go. If you're committed to buying in large quantities, it's best to have a system that can handle it. If you live in a house, you might set up a shelving unit in your garage or basement. You might label the shelves of the items you most often buy; then, if it's empty, a quick glance will tell you what goes in that space.

If you have a big family, big-box stores can be a huge help with your budget; but if you live on your own or in a small space, ask yourself if it's helping. Figure out exactly what you're saving. You don't have to live with paper towels piled up in your living room. Those giant jars of peanut butter that only come in a two-pack can last all year for two people.

Buy Prepared Food

While food prep is obviously about . . . prepping food, there's no need to make it as difficult as possible. Sure, peeled and precut butternut squash may be a bit more expensive than buying it whole, but it's cheaper than eating out. There's no shame in cutting a few corners to give yourself time to get other things done.

Cook Enough for Multiple Meals

Consider ingredients that can be used in multiple meals throughout the week. That chicken you cooked for Taco Tuesday can also be used in chicken noodle soup on Friday. Or the vegetables you roasted for your work lunches can be added to a veggie pizza. It may seem like a lot when you're prepping the foods, but making enough for the whole week is a game changer.

Choose Well-Made, Long-Lasting Containers

Our preference for storage containers is primarily glass with clear tops. They work great for stacking and allow you to easily locate what you're looking for. But plastic definitely works better when you're taking your lunch with you (glass is too heavy) and certainly when kids' lunch boxes are involved. Of course, you can use what you already have. Just make sure that everything is clearly marked and visible, so you don't end up with that random mystery container in the back of the fridge! Kate uses a paint pen to mark things. Ann uses Post-Its.

Sentimental Items

In the kitchen, sentimental items tend to be childhood favorites or things passed down from parents and grandparents. These are the sorts of things that make a house a home. Keep a few items in your working kitchen, but only what makes life easier: that sturdy chef's knife from your mom's house, the mug your grandmother always used and is now your favorite, or your children's baby spoons that are still useful with small jars. If you decide to keep items that are sentimental but not useful, like baby dishes, we recommend boxing them up and putting them with other **Save Forever** items that are stored outside of the kitchen.

Owning Well

Spend on the items you'll use the most.

Appliances

The kitchen provides endless examples of Owning Well. On the high end, there are KitchenAid stand mixers and Vitamix blenders. As we laid out earlier, you have to be realistic about what you're going to use and make **Intentional Investments**. If you bake every week, then saving up for a brand-name stand mixer makes all the sense in the world. If, however, you "bake" a pie at Thanksgiving (meaning you put some pumpkin pie filling in a premade crust), then a less expensive hand mixer is all you need. An Intentional Investment is one that makes the most financial sense for the life *you* live.

Once you've saved up and made the big-time purchase, now is the time to protect your investment. Whether that means storing and carefully packing up your precious crystal, or sending in the warranty on your Vitamix, **Mindful Maintenance** means caring for your purchases so they last a lifetime.

Eco Tips

The kitchen is a great place to make eco-friendly swaps. You can make small changes or big changes, but there are a multitude of things you can do to make your space greener:

- **IN OUR OWN KITCHENS,** we've replaced almost all of the paper towels with Marleys Monsters: UnPaper Towels, which are several cloths on a roll that you can pull apart and use to mop up spills and clean surfaces and then launder as needed.

- **TO REDUCE CONSUMPTION** of single-use plastic, use washable silicone storage bags in place of plastic baggies and beeswax cloths instead of plastic wrap to cover food and bowls.

- **PURCHASE SPONGES MADE OF** either sustainable, biodegradable materials or silicone, which last pretty much forever. So much of our daily trash comes from the kitchen; so

having even one product that you can keep out of the garbage is a huge win.

- **IF YOU AREN'T PREPARED TO INVEST** in new environmentally healthy products, there are inexpensive, tried-and-tested DIY solutions you can assemble at home. For instance, if you mix vinegar, essential oils, and baking soda, you'll have a great, all-purpose surface cleanser.

Keep It Up!

In order to keep your kitchen running smoothly year after year, there are some things you can do every few months or even once a year that will make a big difference. Every so often, take an hour to reorganize your pantry. Do the same ruthless decluttering you did the first time; this time it will result in much less waste. You should also inventory your freezer and see what should be eaten soon or tossed, and what needs to be purchased. If you use wooden cutting boards, they should be oiled a couple of times a year with John Boos Mystery Oil, and good knives should be sharpened once a year.

Bedroom

A peaceful space that supports restful nights and hopeful mornings

A PEACEFUL BEDROOM CAN ONLY HAPPEN when there is a place for everything, and everything is in its place. If your home is a respite from the outside world, your bedroom is a respite from your home. People want their bedrooms to be places of relaxation and calm where they can decompress at the end of the day. Having a calm bedroom supports good sleep habits, which in turn make for a happier life. Since your bedroom is the first thing you see when you wake up in the morning, a clean, clutter-free space sets you up for a more tranquil day.

What happens when you open your eyes and see stacks of clutter, specifically things that don't belong in a bedroom? Mail, laundry to be folded, children's creations, and other general to-dos? There is nothing relaxing or sexy about responsibilities and chores. The first goal for the bedroom is to remove everything that doesn't belong and find a proper home for it.

Most people keep their clothes in their bedroom or in an adjoining closet. If you have the right amount of clothes for the space, putting laundry away will be easy—so that you do it, rather than letting loads of clean laundry pile up on a chair or on your dresser.

The size of the bedroom is less important than having the correct amount of storage. It's much easier to create a peaceful sanctuary if there is a place for everything that is staying in your bedroom.

- **DRESSERS ALLOW FOR EASY STORAGE** of small items like socks, underwear, and T-shirts.
- **A CHEST AT THE END OF THE BED** can hold out-of-season or bulky items.
- **BEDSIDE TABLES WITH DRAWERS** make it easy to organize all the items—glasses, eye masks, book lights, etc.—that would otherwise end up on top of the bedside table and create visual chaos.
- **UNDER-BED STORAGE THAT ACTUALLY FUNCTIONS** is great space for things like linens.

Having closets that are well organized and hold only the items you are currently using means that getting ready for any event, whether work or a black-tie wedding, is easy. The lack of stress lightens your feelings about the actual event, too, because you didn't get ready under a cloud.

If your bedroom is full of things that don't belong, it's like you're trying to make your life more difficult: "Please, please, make sure I don't have enough room to put my clean clothes away. Please make it impossible to find my favorite jeans. Oh, please, make it harder than it needs to be for me to go to the gym, because that isn't hard enough already. One last thing: My mornings aren't stressful enough, so please help me to take an extra twenty minutes to get dressed so I can be a sweaty mess before I even leave the house."

You might think that nobody would choose to live in that sort of bedroom—but by electing not to get organized, it's exactly what you're choosing.

How Do You Use Your Bedroom?

In a dream world, your bedroom would be used only for sleep, relaxing, and sex; but we know all too well that many people have not only a workstation in there, but exercise equipment as well.

As long as you or your partner actually uses the office and the exercise equipment—and there is no other logical place those things can reasonably go—they should stay. But if the exercise bike has become a large catchall for your clothes, and you haven't used it for exercise in a year, then consider letting it go.

Do you save this room for sleep or use it for exercise and work as well?

Make
your room
a calm and
tidy refuge.

If you have little ones at home, you may want to consider making your bedroom a kid-free zone. That takes courage and discipline. By making your room off-limits to children, you are carving out a space for yourself and your spouse. It's much more likely to stay tidy (and sexy!) without the family parade coming through and hanging out in there every day.

Let's also consider the bedroom closet, and how it's used:

- **DO YOU SHARE A CLOSET** with your spouse or partner?
- **DO YOU HAVE MORE FORMAL WORK CLOTHES** that are distinct from your everyday clothes?
- **HOW OFTEN DO YOU DO LAUNDRY?**
- **DO YOU HAVE A WALK-IN CLOSET,** or do you have a reach-in closet with a simple bar and shelf?

The answers to these questions will help you make smart decisions about how and where you store your clothing.

PRO TIP:

Velvet Hangers

Swap out your wire and plastic hangers for matching velvet hangers. We know a lot of organizing products can be expensive and changing out your hangers might seem like the definition of waste. But velvet hangers can make a huge difference in how your closet functions and how it looks. Velvet hangers are thinner than wood hangers, so you gain space; plus your clothing stays on them nicely, unlike on plastic hangers, where items keep slipping off. "Full hangers" (with the bar across the bottom) work better than "shirt hangers" because the latter get tangled among the other hangers. Keeping a few wooden hangers for suits and sports jackets is a good idea.

Ask a Friend

Consider enlisting the help of a good friend when you tackle your clothes. It's a huge help to have a friend there because they can rehang and refold while you try things on. Don't choose a friend or family member who has ever said unkind things about your clothes or your body. Choose the person who is always happy to see you and gives you genuine compliments. Offer to help her if she's willing to help you. Choose someone you can laugh with, because it can be embarrassing and sometimes a little shameful to be confronted with a huge number of items you don't want. Some will have tags on them. You don't need a guilt-producing friend here. You need one who's quick to laugh and to cheer you on through the process.

SORT AND DECIDE

You might think the chaos in your bedroom is because you don't have enough space. That's rarely the problem. We've seen New York City bedrooms with just a tiny bedside table on each side and no room for other furniture that worked perfectly. That's only a 10′ x 10′ room! We're guessing your bedroom is larger than that—so why isn't it the sanctuary of your dreams? The problem is caused by all the things that do not belong there.

ITEMS WE OFTEN FIND IN BEDROOMS THAT DON'T BELONG IN THE BEDROOM:

- New purchases and returns
- Donation bags and Save Forever bins
- Toiletries
- Household linens unrelated to this bedroom
- Stray papers (such as school forms, homework, and unopened mail)
- Pens and stationery (unless you have a home office in your bedroom)

ITEMS THAT DO BELONG IN THE BEDROOM:

- Clothes
- Shoes
- Jewelry
- Books
- Linens for this bedroom

ORGANIZE YOUR CLOTHES

Learning to declutter and organize clothes is a skill that will serve you well over the years to come. Whether for closets or dressers, the trick to sorting clothes is basically the same.

If you have sentimental saves tucked in your drawers that are not clothes, gather all those together and place them in a box or a laundry basket for now and we'll deal with them later. Our hope is that, when you're done, your dresser drawers only have clothes or jewelry.

We have had clients who got bogged down with way too much stuff. But, once they understood how to declutter, they became unstoppable. They often got rid of way more than they kept and now report to us that they are still buying less.

Underwear

We realize in each of these categories you may have cumulatively spent a fortune, so "less expensive" might not seem to apply—but if you've spent a fortune on bras, we guarantee you've spent even more on dresses, shoes, and bags. So, relatively speaking, this stuff is inexpensive.

Some of our clients have way too much underwear and some don't have enough. There is no reason to run out of clean underwear—but more than three weeks' worth, or more than twenty-one pairs of underwear, borders on excessive. Thirty pairs should be the absolute max and fewer than ten could make your laundry life more challenging than it needs to be. There is no need to hang on to uncomfortable or tattered underwear. Just don't.

Visibility is key to not overpurchasing!

In all things, it's best to find your favorite brand and stick with it. Make a note of your size in your phone and then you can order more as needed. (This is especially true with the brand and size of bras. Sizing is inconsistent across brands, and if you want to order online it's nearly impossible if you can no longer read the size and brand on an old tag. That means a time-wasting trip to the store.)

Speaking of time-wasting, is it a time suck to fold your underwear? It might be, but it's also nice to open that drawer first thing in the morning and see everything in order.

Accept Sunk Costs

The more expensive something is, the harder it will be to part with, whether you wear it or not. Be prepared for this and remember that the money is gone. That term **Sunk Cost** comes in handy here. Say to yourself, "What's done is done" and "Oh well," as many times as you need to in order to let things go. This is one of the reasons why we start with the less expensive items such as socks, T-shirts, and underwear. Tackle lower-priced brands (like things you picked up at Target or Old Navy) and then move on to high-end, special items. In all categories of clothing except these (socks and underwear), everything should be tried on in order to decide if you really want to keep it.

Socks

It's as mysterious to us as it is to everybody else—how do pairs get separated, never to be reunited? We can't explain it, so we just accept that it happens. We've worked in homes with huge bags of single socks that had clearly been collected over many years. We hate to be hope-dashers, but we're doing it here—throw those single socks in the garbage or in the textile donation bag. In order to prevent the waste in the future, always buy the same brand in each category, whether it's gym socks or dress socks or no-show socks. When one goes missing, put its twin in the place where you'll always look and when it inevitably happens again to another pair, you'll have a match.

So now all the smaller, less expensive items have been handled. All the "keep" items are refolded and back in the drawers or perhaps bins on the closet shelves if you don't have a dresser. You're halfway to becoming an expert at decluttering clothes!

Bras

How many bras should you keep? This partly depends on the size of the space where you keep them and how realistic you feel you need to be about what you will and won't continue to wear. After a certain age and after being married or with your partner for more than a certain amount of time, how many fancy, uncomfortable bras do you really wear? We don't want to be dream crushers but . . .

See how we didn't put an age or an amount of time on those sentences above? Maybe you still swing from the chandeliers at age sixty after thirty years of marriage. You have our profound respect; the rest of us mortals have less need for the lacy lingerie and more need for the bras that don't cut into us, slide up, or slide off our shoulders, and generally do their job without reminding us all day that we have a bra on. If you find that perfect bra, order three to six of them and get rid of the others. Seriously, throw the ones that hurt you into the donation bag. The three-to-six range is because some people wear a bra only once before washing it. Other people find that crazy and wear them for days without washing them. Other people say bras have to "rest" for at least a day between wears to maintain the support. We're not getting into this debate. You can take it up with the internet and make up your own mind; and then purchase and wash according to your deeply held beliefs.

T-Shirts

Working through the drawers, you've purged underwear and bras, so we can now move on to T-shirts. Separate them into dressier, more expensive T-shirts and then the others that may have writing on them or perhaps a stack of not-great-looking ones that you wear to the gym. (Though

Be ruthless when deciding which beloved tees to keep.

it's a mystery to us why you would wear something unattractive when you'll be seeing yourself in the mirror at the gym for the next hour? Be nice to yourself!)

Carry on with the same system of subcategories and like-with-like. Start with four T-shirts that are definitely staying and four that are definitely going. Carry on through all the stacks and, as always, be ruthless. If you have some that you can't decide about yet, just set those to the side. Always set anything to the side that slows you down in any category of decluttering and purging. Once you put away the definite "keeps" and bag up the definite "goes," the "to-be-decided" pile can be resolved much more easily. The space you have and how you want it to look and function will help you decide if you want to cram those five T-shirts back into the drawer or let them go. When you're done, you can actually see the ones you truly like and want to wear.

Workout Clothes

Unless you work out like a fiend and have to take your laundry some distance to the laundromat, you don't need ten sports bras. We occasionally have clients who don't do their own laundry because the cleaner or housekeeper does it. If they only come in once a week and you work out every day, then maybe you do need seven to ten sports bras. For the rest of us, when we manage to drag our butts to the gym or go for a run a couple of times a week, we can just throw our sports bra in the washer with our workout clothes when we get home. Not washing your workout clothes immediately (or at least rinsing them with cold water) is part of the reason why they get so stinky. Once they get stinky, you can't easily get rid of the smell and then you buy new ones. Owning the right amount of workout clothing and taking good care of it saves time, money, and effort.

Keep this in mind when you are purchasing new workout clothes. Brands keep developing better and better materials, so many people keep purchasing new items. Be reasonable about how many pairs of leggings you really need when you consistently do laundry.

PRO TIP:

Don't Forget Stashed Clothes

If you've overflowed your own room and taken clothes to other parts of the house like a guest-room closet or your children's closets (their clothes are so small you can add to it and they won't even notice, right?), go get those clothes now. Do you have out-of-season clothes or maybe shoes in those under-the-bed storage boxes? Pull those out, too.

Dresses, Suits, Skirts, Dress Pants, and Sweaters

Pull out a whole category and put like with like. As you're learning, this is the number-one rule of decluttering. Your brain will not accept the madness of the dress, suit, or sweater situation until they're all in one place. Once they are all in one place you can start to categorize into "definitely keep," "definitely go," and "to be decided."

Grouping likes with likes in the closet makes getting dressed a cinch!

Do you need all of these shirts?
Try them on to be sure they're worth keeping.

Let's use sweaters as an example. Choose the four you like the most and set them aside. Next, choose four sweaters you know you will never wear again, and put those in the donate bag. I can hear one or maybe two of you saying, "Wait. I only have eight sweaters in total." You can put this book down and pat yourself on the back. You are an organizational expert, and you should probably send your résumé to us at Done & Done Home.

For the rest of you, keep sorting in this way, but reduce the number from four to two—so now keep two, donate two, and so on, until there are no sweaters left on the bed. Now try everything on in the "definitely keep" pile and take a good look in the mirror.

Be ruthless. Now that you've tried them on and seen the whole "keep" stack, can you get rid of a couple more? If the "keep" pile is more than twenty sweaters, imagine that someone is paying you to donate them. Which one or two would you part with now? Maybe a couple more can go.

Dresses, pants, jeans, skirts, and even jackets and coats can all be reduced with this method.

Once you've decided which ones you think you're keeping, try them on. *All of them*. We've spent lots of time with our female clients in their undies. Trying on has to be done. Keeping without trying the items on is a fool's game. You'll keep way more than you'll ever wear again. Once you decide what you're keeping, rehang those in your closet and move on to your next section.

PRO TIP:

Donating Men's Clothes Is Important

If you or your partner is a tall man (over six feet) the donation centers want your clothes. For tall men who are looking to purchase clothes, especially for job interviews, it's important that the arm length and inseam of trousers are not too short. This is also true for larger shoe sizes. These are some of the least donated items that can make the most difference to someone else.

Shoes

Clients always ask us how many is too many pairs of shoes. We can safely say the number you have now is too many! How do we know? You're reading our book so we can bet you have too many shoes! Be ruthless when clearing out your shoe collection—not only because shoes are big and take up space, but also because they tend to get worn out if you wear them often and may need to be replaced. And what about the shoes in perfect condition? They might look great because you don't wear them . . . and that's another reason to eliminate them.

Buying on Sale Is Still Buying

JOAN HAD A MASSIVE CLOSET filled with clothes that didn't suit her, a wide range of sizes that didn't fit her, and many things she didn't even like. It turned out that the high she got from buying items on sale was the primary driving force. She hadn't built a wardrobe so much as she simply "saved money" buying discounted items.

First, we culled the piles, bagging all the things that didn't fit her currently and weren't within a size of the dream of wearing them. A woman who wears a size 10 may wear a size 8 or a size 12 but is unlikely to wear a 4 or a 6 in any brand. (Nor is she likely to wear a size 14.) Next, we had her try every single item that she wanted to keep. This always reveals the discrepancy in sizing from brand to brand. Even though, generally speaking, Joan wore a size 8 in jeans, nobody wants to do the "pull and hop" to get into their jeans.

We kept on with this for hours—and finally, everything that remained was able to fit in her closet and drawers. Before we put things away, we took pictures of outfits that excited her.

We put the items away using a system that gave order to her clothes. She could now find a blouse first thing in the morning and decide with ease what to do with it when she returned in the evening.

Because Joan's problems began at the store, we also helped her make an inventory of all the clothes she kept. We encouraged her to maintain this list and refer to it often. When you are about to buy more clothes, it can be helpful to know you already have four cream-colored blouses or six black sweaters.

We understand that this is difficult for lots of people. Shoes and boots are expensive, and well-made shoes don't wear out quickly, which makes us feel we should keep them, even if they've gone out of style. Also as adults we don't often outgrow them—unless, like us, your feet grew during pregnancy; that's very common. What can we say? There is simply no reason to keep shoes you don't wear. This may be painful. A woman who wears a size 9 shoe is never again going to be a size 8. You can't get your shoe size back after having a baby the way you can get your waist back. You already knew this—intellectually, anyway. But the shoes you don't wear *are still in your closet.* Let's change that.

Go get them all now and lay them out in subcategories (boots, flip-flops, heels, etc.) and then like-with-like so that strappy heels are separate from regular heels, and dress booties are separate from snow boots. Try very hard to keep fantasy at bay here! If you haven't worn them in the last year, you probably aren't ever going to wear them again.

Be as ruthless as possible and know that you are going to buy another pair of shoes in the future—we guarantee it—so even if you do get rid of what you perceive as one too many, another pair will pop up to take its place. You can let go with the knowledge that shoe designers and manufacturers will continue to make the toe narrower next season or the heel chunkier, so soon your current shoes won't look right and then you'll buy more. Forever and ever, until you die wearing hospital socks. Seriously, get a grip on yourself and let those old shoes go. Take a photo of all the shoes that you're donating and look at the photo each time you go to purchase another pair.

Sentimental Items

What can you do with clothes that mean something emotionally but have no daily use? Hoodies from college and old Levi's—not the good, vintage ones that you can sell, but the weird bootleg ones with the low-rise zipper from 2002? How about those vacation-spot sweatshirts, or shorts and bathing suits from that perfect summer at the beach? What about the T-shirts you

PRO TIP:
What Are You Wearing?

Don't keep shoes you don't wear regularly! Often, clients hire us to help with the home of a deceased loved one, and we've cleared out plenty of homes where the woman who died hadn't worn anything other than slippers or comfy sneakers in years—and yet, right there in the closet, were thirty pairs of heels and dress shoes. And always, always the wedding pumps. Must we really hang on to a pair of shoes we wore for seven hours, fifty years ago?

Save a few dear items, and store them where they can be seen and enjoyed.

collected at concerts and marathons? This is hard for many people. You don't wear them . . . but you don't want to throw them away, either.

Our suggestion is first to pare down your collection, eliminating any previously nostalgic clothes that no longer have meaning to you. It's OK to recognize that sometimes sentiment fades. Then pack the remaining items and move them out of your working wardrobe. You're creating a Save Forever collection, which doesn't belong in your closet or in drawers where you keep the items you wear regularly. That's your prime clothing real estate! And here's a tip: If you don't like the idea of your special memories living in a box, you can send those T-shirts and other clothing items to a quiltmaker, who can be found on Etsy. They will create an attractive quilt that you can keep, and use, forever.

Wedding Dresses

A wedding dress is usually packed in a large heirloom box that takes up a lot of space in the closet. This is especially challenging if you're an apartment dweller with little storage space. But donating it is also hard! Your dress was likely expensive, maybe even the single most expensive item of clothing you've ever purchased, and the emotional attachment is huge. Some brides fantasize that one day their daughter will wear the dress when she gets married.

This *could* happen, but in our experience it's very unlikely. Yes, a modern bride may incorporate something from her mother's dress into her dress— but you don't need to keep a huge box in every home you live in for thirty or forty years just so your daughter can snip off a bit of lace or a satin rose and have it sewn into her dress.

The reality is, wedding dresses are sentimental cloth taking up very real space for a very long period of time. No judgment on this one—at least not from Ann, because guess whose wedding dress is at her house taking up precious space in her closet? Kate's!

Kate was completely unemotional about her dress and tried to sell it very soon after her wedding. She also offered to give it to her cousins and friends, but they wanted to pick out their own dresses, just as she had. She tried to donate it to a few sites that specialized in wedding dresses that people can buy at a huge discount, but none of those sites needed dresses—they needed buyers. Kate felt she'd done all she could and was prepared to drop it off at Goodwill. That was a bridge too far for Ann, so Kate said, "OK, then you keep it." That was almost ten years ago, and Ann is no closer to putting the dress in the donation pile.

See, we're just like you. We're not perfect either.

Jewelry

Your everyday jewelry is best stored in clear, sectioned cases while valuable jewelry should be kept in a safe. The standard jewelry box tends to be lined in dark material and doesn't have enough divided areas, so necklaces get twisted and earrings don't stay together. If you have drawer space you can put the jewelry in there, but if not, they look pretty stacked on top of the dresser.

Clear, sectioned trays mean no more tangled necklaces!

Imagine a closet where things are as easy to put away as they are to find.

Keep Your Bedroom and Your Closets Running Smoothly

As in other areas of the home, the trick to maintaining order in the bedroom is to keep only the things that can fit and to use proper storage solutions so it's easy to both find and put away those things. It also helps to have exactly what you need to access every inch of storage space; so keep a stepladder in the closet if you can't easily reach the top shelves.

PRO TIP:
Play This Game

Our absolute favorite game is called "Wear It All Day or Give It Away." If you're unsure about an item of clothing or jewelry, or an accessory, wear it for an entire day. This forces you to make a decision. No one wants to be stuck in an ill-fitting, out-of-date, hot mess of an uncomfortable outfit!

We invented this game while working with a client who was particularly attached to her clothes. She hadn't ever gone up or down in size, which she was rightfully proud of, because she worked hard to maintain her figure. She also spent a lot of money on clothes and loved to shop. The result was that every closet in her very large apartment was packed with clothes. But she was selling her apartment, so she needed her closets pared down and as close to empty as possible.

We worked with her for days and made great progress in the other areas of her home, but the clothes situation was seem-ingly impossible. She didn't want to get rid of anything. She insisted it was all too high-quality to donate, but the truth was, it was also far too dated to sell or wear. We finally found our solution when she was telling us about a particularly nice suit she wanted to keep. She said she would *definitely* wear it again, no problem at all, even though she had bought it in the 1980s and it had shoulder pads and a very narrow skirt. Kate asked her to put it on, leave the house, and walk up the block to the corner Starbucks and get us all some coffee. She didn't say anything for a minute. Then she started laughing and couldn't stop. The image of herself in that outdated suit finally showed her how crazy it was to hold on to things that she was never, ever going to wear—and that not doing a proper purge would cost her a lot of money, because her home wouldn't show as well if it were cluttered.

Myth Busted

"It's wrong to store things under the bed."

IN A PERFECT WORLD WE WOULD ALL HAVE beautiful walk-in closets with so much space we couldn't fill them—but that's rarely the case, so we use the space we have. When storing under a bed, it's ideal if the platform itself has drawers, or if the whole mattress lifts up on a hydraulic platform with easy access to all that space. This helps you avoid the situation where you're lying flat on your stomach pulling out those plastic bags full of shoes and avoiding dust bunnies at the same time. If your bed is low down so plastic storage bags are the only things that fit, consider using risers (like the ones sold to college students) to increase the height of the under-bed space. Then get proper bins with good-fitting lids so no dust gets inside.

We also recommend a couple of hampers in or near the closet for laundry—one for regular laundry and a smaller one for handwashing. It also helps to have a bag for dry cleaning and a bag for donations. When you've tried on a shirt a few times and haven't chosen to wear it, you are unlikely to choose it in the future—so pop that in the donation bag while whispering to yourself, "Release this to the universe" and "Sunk Costs."

If you have the setup to choose whether you use shelves or drawers for certain items, use your drawers for things that are small and don't fold well (like undies), or don't stay folded because of the material they're made of (like gym clothes). Use your shelves for things that stack more easily, like jeans and sweaters.

A word on file folding—we would be remiss not to mention something that we learned from Marie Kondo: All hail the file fold. It's truly a miracle. Once you learn how to do it and it becomes part of your everyday life, you'll wonder how in the world you lived without this most basic skill. If file folding is mysterious to you for any article of clothing, just head over to YouTube—there are a million videos!

We aren't beholden to color coding because we don't want to make any of this harder or more time consuming than it already is, but we do use a basic light-to-dark system for hanging clothes with patterns at the end of the row. We also hang sleeveless first and then short-sleeve items, and finally long-sleeve items; so, when "reading" left to right, the shirts would be gently color-coded within sleeveless and then short sleeves, starting again with light to dark and then on to the long-sleeve shirts.

File folding prevents clothes from getting lost at the bottom of the stack.

Owning Well

Less really is more, in a well-curated wardrobe.

Fewer Things, Greater Care

The saying goes "Less but better," and this is a great lesson to remember in dealing with your closet. As you follow our steps and you learn to watch how much you buy, you'll also be able to buy things you truly love. When you take the time to make Intentional Investments regarding your wardrobe, you'll find things that last and remain stylish for years. Try to avoid trendy cuts, colors, and materials. Whether it's a navy blazer for work or a pair of tried-and-true Levi's, classic clothes will last for much longer than a single season. This also applies to shoes, accessories, and jewelry, and if you're unsure about the price of a high-quality purchase, remember that if something is going to last for years, your cost per wear will make the price much more reasonable.

Once you have the wardrobe of your dreams, you need to take care of all your items with

Mindful Maintenance. Regardless of what the tag says, dry cleaning is not always the best option. Often hand-washing and air-drying delicate clothing is a better choice. The chemicals used at the dry cleaners may be harsh and ultimately shorten the life span of your investments. Obviously, this doesn't apply to things like suits and blazers; but if you do a little research, you'll be shocked by how much you can wash at home.

To be completely truthful, we must admit that your workout clothes will not last forever. If you wear them consistently for working out, not just running to the grocery store, they will eventually need to be replaced. The good news is, we have a hack for keeping them smelling fresh—Head & Shoulders shampoo! We're not exactly sure about the science of it all (it has something to do with the zinc); we just know it works. Put a capful in your wash with all of your sweaty workout clothes and you won't have to trash perfectly good things simply because you couldn't get the smell out.

Research brands before you buy any article of clothing. Many companies have quality guarantees, so you know you're getting a quality product, and some are now even offering recycling programs! It may be worth the extra money to know your clothes will last and will be taken care of at the end of their life cycle.

Eco Tips

"Fast fashion" is an incredibly problematic business model for the entire planet. The best way to make your closet eco-friendly is to reduce the amount of clothes you're buying. Stop impulse shopping and carefully consider whether you actually need a new item and if you're truly going to wear it. We can teach you how to declutter your closet effectively, but the goal is to not have to do a giant cull every few months. The less you buy, the less you have to let go of—and the less that ends up polluting the planet.

Some other great environmentally friendly options are to shop at your local thrift stores or at secondhand fashion services like thredUP and Poshmark.

Keep It Up!

Once a month or so when you're putting laundry away, try and take a few extra minutes to organize your drawers. If it seems like an overwhelming task, you may have too much in that drawer. The hardest thing about organizing is having too much stuff for the space you have. Once you've done the decluttering and put everything back in its place, it will be much easier to keep everything tidy; but if you keep shopping and don't edit quarterly, things will get tight. If you find yourself putting clean clothes on top of the dresser or you leave them in the laundry basket instead of putting them away, it's a clue that the drawers may be too full again. Pull out a few items you know you haven't worn since you did the big clean-out and put them in the donation bag.

Bathroom

A rejuvenating space where you begin
each morning and end each day

A STREAMLINED BATHROOM is the secret weapon to a successful day. It's where we do so much of our self-care, so if the space is well organized and you are able to take care of yourself for even five minutes, first thing in the morning, you'll feel better all day.

An organized bathroom also makes getting out the door in the morning looking pulled-together a snap. It supports ease and efficiency, which reduces everyday stress. So much of what it takes to look good each day happens in the bathroom (blow-drying, skin care, makeup, etc.). If this space is cluttered and dysfunctional, the morning will be difficult.

When there are children in the home, the spa-like experience of an evening bath may feel out of reach, but there is always hope. In an organized bathroom, the likelihood of a lit candle and a nice soak may be possible, if you don't have to gather up the whales, boats, and other bath toys before you even fill the tub. Baby Beluga will be tucked away in his spot right after the children are finished bathing.

If your bathroom is chaotic, many small issues may occur on a daily basis to make life harder:

- **FORGOT TO PICK UP NEW DEODORANT?** Let's hope it's not August.
- **DIDN'T ORDER YOUR NEW CONTACTS ON TIME?** I guess you'll be wearing your old glasses.
- **DIDN'T REALIZE YOU WERE OUT OF CONCEALER?** There's no disguising the exhaustion now.
- **CAN'T FIND THE HAIR SPRAY THAT ACTUALLY WORKS?** Another bad hair day it is.

Bathrooms come in all shapes and sizes, but in general they are smaller than other rooms in the home and also tend to accumulate a ton of "product"—together, a perfect storm for disorganization.

How Do You Use Your Bathroom?

Create a list of how you, and anyone you share your bathroom with, use the space:

- **DO YOU SHOWER** in the morning or at night?
- **DO YOU WEAR MAKEUP** every day or almost never?
- **DO YOU PUT YOUR MAKEUP ON** in the bathroom?
- **DO YOU BLOW-DRY** and straighten your hair at home?
- **ARE YOU A PERSON WHO LOVES USING LOTIONS** and potions? Or are you a person who loves buying them more than using them?
- **WHEN'S THE LAST TIME YOU DID A FACE MASK** or a pedicure at home?

The answers to these questions will help you make smart decisions about how you organize and store your bathroom products.

Do you come here to escape or is it all business?

SORT AND DECIDE

Unless you have a huge bathroom where you can sort everything on the counters and floor, use a laundry basket to gather all the items and products from your bathroom drawers and cabinets, and move *everything* to a place where you can spread out. It may take a few trips, but it's worth it to be able to see all of the small items. Alert: You may not want to do this sorting in your bedroom because bathroom products are often liquid—including lotions and shampoos that may spill and makeup and nail polish that can stain.

Bathroom products are especially important to sort like-with-like. Lotions, medicines, hair products, cleansers, etc., should be grouped into sections on the floor or counters. Within each category you then create subcategories. For example, hair products become hair sprays, shampoos, conditioners, gels, dry shampoo, hair dye, brushes, combs, etc. You may quickly see where your buying problems are.

Take a quick pass over each category and subcategory; then grab everything that you know you don't use, and aren't going to use, ever. If it is open or expired, it is actual garbage unless you know someone who loves products and wants your castoffs. In other words, there is not a market for donating used or expired products.

Think hard before making a box or bag for another person in your life. Only give nice products. It's just not a great practice to dump the stuff you can't deal with having purchased onto someone else. If you have good, barely used items or things that are unopened, consider gifting those to a friend or family member who would truly appreciate it.

We know—we know! Some of you may be thinking, *Wait a minute, I always give everything I don't want to my sister/friend/mother, and she loves it.* Maybe. Or maybe she can't say no because she doesn't want to hurt your feelings. Or maybe she's like many of our clients who somehow became the receiver of all unwanted stuff in the family—and though it makes her life hard she doesn't know how to stop saying yes. What we're saying is try

PRO TIP:

Small Things Add Up

We all love those tiny, pocket-sized supplies that come from airplanes and hotels when we travel, and we like to take them home with us, either for the next time we travel, or for guests at our home, or "just in case." But we so rarely use them. Though they are small individually, all together they take up a lot of space. If you don't want them to go to waste, you can make give-away kits by filling small bags with a toothbrush, shampoo, body wash, and mouthwash, and then donate the kits to a local homeless shelter. If you want to keep some, put them in a bin or basket that is clearly labeled. When the bin is filled, you'll know it's time to stop bringing them home from hotels.

your hardest to be 100 percent responsible for the items you purchased without relying on others to bail you out of the situation you're currently in.

Some people are super hopeful that a different hair spray is going to handle the humidity once and for all. But alas, they all sort of work . . . but none of them are perfect, so you keep buying new ones. If you only do this a couple of times a year but never throw them away, you can easily end up with four to six different hair sprays, maybe more. Pick the one you like the most and then one more. Put all the ones you aren't choosing in the to-be-decided area. You'll come back to those later because, as we outlined in the kitchen section with the coffee maker, if you have three hair sprays you haven't chosen once this year, that's 1,095 times you chose a different one.

BEAUTY PRODUCTS

Makeup, cosmetics, lotions, and potions can be expensive, which makes it harder to accept when they don't work out for you. It's hard to put bottles and jars of hope, especially the pricey ones, in the garbage bag.

- **THAT SHADE OF NAIL POLISH THAT LOOKED NEW AND EXCITING** at the store but now looks crazy? It's never going to look any less crazy. It was a mistake.
- **THE LIPSTICK THAT IS NOWHERE NEAR THE COLOR YOU USUALLY WEAR.** You hung on to it because you didn't want to waste money. Unfortunately, the money's gone and the lipstick is hanging around reminding you that you misspent.

These are the Sunk Costs of beauty. There's no shame in trying new things. We all do it. The problem is in not accepting when it doesn't work. Once you've decided against a product and moved on, you very rarely change your mind about it and go back. You might try it again—but you won't actually leave the house wearing it. If you know exactly what you have and what works for you, you're so much less likely to waste money on things like this again.

Which of these items really works for you?

Small-Space Strategies

EMMA SHARES A SMALL, SINGLE-SINK BATHROOM with her husband and four kids, so we made the space work for her by storing very little in there. After a massive declutter, we put stacking bins under the bathroom sink for necessities and added a freestanding tower with bins to store everyday products. Emma now says the intimate moments brushing her teeth with her kids are some of the best parts of the day.

More than in any other room, using vertical space in the bathroom helps so much. A freestanding rack with bins can provide a lot of storage space. A deeper, taller medicine cabinet or storage over the toilet can be game changers.

Keep Your Bathroom Running Smoothly

Once you've done the great clear-out of all the things you don't use, you can begin to organize all the things you want to keep in bins in your bathroom.

We recommend clear plastic bins for the bathroom—and though we often don't use lids on bins, they help when it comes to cosmetics and toiletries. Inexpensive plastic shoebox bins with lids are narrow and stack well. They're easy to see through and easy to label. If you have the space, keep categories as small as possible. If your space is limited, you may need to use one slightly larger bin; then your "hair" box can hold sprays and mousse as well as brushes, combs, and straighteners.

We also suggest more bins in the bathroom than in other areas of the home, mostly because it's easy to keep track of what you already have so you don't buy more. It's harder to lie to yourself about how much you have of any sort of product when it's grouped together. Storing lipstick all over the place means you can easily have twenty and not know it. It isn't obvious how many you actually have until they are in one small bin together.

Plastic bins can bring sanity to a once chaotic cabinet.

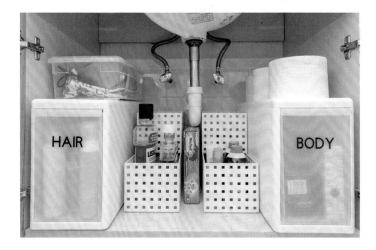

Myth Busted

"Vanities are old-fashioned."

WHENEVER POSSIBLE GET YOUR MAKEUP OUT OF YOUR BATHROOM. Freestanding makeup vanities may seem like a thing of the past, like sitting down in the dining room and eating off the good china, but honestly, a vanity in the bedroom can be a game changer. It can help clear up space in your bathroom for the things that actually need to be there and allow your partner to get ready while you are doing your makeup. Also, each individual bit of makeup is small—a mascara, a lipstick, a bottle of foundation. They get lost under the bathroom sink or in that closet in the bathroom that's really meant for towels and hair dryers.

A vanity keeps you honest. The drawers are rarely deep. You can see everything you actually use. It doesn't hold such a large collection that you get overwhelmed just looking at it. A good solution is to put your everyday makeup in your vanity and keep your backup in a bin in the bathroom. One bin.

Vanities can be in your bedroom, in your bathroom if it's big enough, or even just outside the bathroom door. Kate's vanity is on the landing right outside the bathroom.

Owning Well

Buying fewer, high-quality items can save you money and time in the long run.

Products, Products, Products

Many of the things we use in the bathroom —hair dryers, straighteners, curling irons, makeup brushes—come in a wide range of prices. You can pick up a hair dryer or a straightener for a song, but as always, the question is, what's it going to cost you in the long run? In our experience, it's absolutely worth making Intentional Investments by saving up to buy the high-end products in this category. They'll last for years and years, and they'll work as advertised. That hair straightener will actually straighten your hair—what a concept!

Often we buy cosmetics and beauty products to solve a problem (frizzy hair, dry skin, blemishes) and somehow it seems more products should do the trick when in actual fact investing in one great product usually works better. It seems scary to overspend on toiletries, so try out samples of new things first.

Makeup brushes are one of the things that you can end up buying over and over again. But if you buy quality brushes and take care of them with Mindful Maintenance, you may literally never have to buy them again. Experts suggest cleaning them every two weeks or whenever you see visible buildup. There are products you can buy to clean them, but baby shampoo will also do the trick!

When you're cleaning those makeup brushes, don't forget your straighteners, curling irons, and hairbrushes—they all need consistent attention as well. Mark your new cosmetics on the bottom with the date as soon as you get them home, so you'll know how long you've had them.

Eco Tips

Bathroom products mostly use plastic packaging and are harder to recycle than an empty can of soda. There are some great brands working to reduce plastic use in toiletries with everything from toothpaste tablets and bar shampoo to reusable cotton pads and bamboo toothbrushes. A few simple switches can make a world of difference on environmental impact.

Keep It Up!

Months after the big clear-out, there will come a time when you can't find something you're looking for in the bathroom that you know you bought recently. Those Band-Aids, that shaving cream, that lipstick are all here somewhere. That's a signal that the order you created is coming undone. Find a little bit of time and put everything back in its right place. If you live with others and share the bathroom, it's guaranteed that it won't stay exactly how you set it up after the decluttering, but it doesn't mean it has to be left to implode. Restoring order in the bathroom every month or so takes almost no time; but if you don't do it right away, soon it will take hours to make it right.

Entry
Spaces

Efficient mudrooms and front hall closets
that make coming and going a breeze

IF THE ENTRY SPACES OF YOUR HOME—whether mudroom, front hall closet, or just a simple drop zone—are well organized, then you can go out into the world confidently prepared for your life.

If these areas are packed with things that don't need to be there (boxes of returns, gifts, wrapping paper, items for donation, holiday decorations, light bulbs, batteries, etc.), then the other items that do need to be there can't fit. It also means that they won't function the way they were designed to. This has real consequences:

- **CAN'T FIND YOUR KEYS?** Kids are late to school.
- **CAN'T FIND THE LEASH?** No one is walking the dog.

The tension caused by looking for items you need in order to leave the house creates an unpleasant atmosphere for all. But when everything you need to get out the door is actually in your entry space:

- **YOU WASTE NO TIME LOOKING** for an umbrella on a rainy day.
- **YOU ARE NEVER DRESSED IN THE WRONG COAT** or jacket, no matter what the weather is.
- **CHILDREN KNOW WHERE TO FIND** and leave their backpacks, shoes, and jackets.

Fixing these spaces so they work for your family means that these daily stresses won't be part of your life. Entry space organization is a question of who lives in your home and how you live. Perhaps you live in a warm-weather climate and much of this doesn't even apply. Whatever your story is, know that the truth of it dictates what stays, what goes, and how you manage the space.

How Do You Use Your Entry Spaces?

Depending on whether you have just a front hall closet, a well-designed mudroom, or an entryway with no extra space at all, you'll want to ask yourself the same questions:

- **ARE THERE THINGS IN THIS SPACE NOW** that have nothing to do with coming and going?
- **ARE THERE ITEMS MISSING FROM HERE** that would make my life easier, but they can't fit?
- **CAN THE CHILDREN—IF THERE ARE ANY—PUT THINGS AWAY** by themselves? Can they reach? Are there hooks and bins to make it easier for them?
- **DO THE ITEMS NEEDED FOR REGULAR ACTIVITIES** (e.g., dog walking) have their own bins or hooks?
- **ARE YOU A FAMILY WHO LEAVES SHOES BY THE FRONT DOOR?** If so, is there a storage system that contains them?

Keep in mind that clear answers to these questions will help you plan how to best utilize the space.

Is this where you bundle up? Drop your bags? Receive guests?

SORT AND DIVIDE

Front hall closet items are difficult to get rid of for the usual reasons. They're often expensive and there is the possibility that you may need, or feel you may need, the formal coat and the fancy winter boots. There could be a winter wedding or a funeral, and what then? Are you going to put on your Uniqlo or Patagonia puffer jacket and head to the church or synagogue? Well, yes, probably you are—but then, you hear your mother's voice in your head telling you to make an effort. So, the camel hair coat and the lined trench coat stay in the closet, even though you haven't worn either in years.

Now is the time to purge. If you have both a front hall closet and a mud-room, these two areas should be done in tandem because the items they hold are related.

Categories to consider:

- Coats
- Boots and shoes
- Winter gear (hats, gloves, scarves)
- Bags and backpacks
- Umbrellas
- Sporting gear
- Dog gear
- Sunglasses
- Sunscreen and bug spray

PRO TIP:

Donation Bags

Do you have donation bags sitting at the bottom of a closet that you've been meaning to drop off for a year? Now is the time to pull them out of the closet and gather all the donatable items together.

To declutter, first group the items by the person who uses them. If it's only you, carry on the way we did in every other room and group like-with-like using subcategories to see what you actually have—coats all together and then subcategories by either use (raincoats and jackets) or fabric (winter wool, down, etc.)

Put all of the items of a spouse or partner in a separate pile; if you have kids, put each child's things in their own separate pile. If your spouse is available, ask them to go through their coats and jackets and, if they're not, consider sending a quick set of photos to them via text and ask for a thumbs-up or thumbs-down so you can handle the

Besides coats and boots, mudrooms can contain other useful everyday items.

Myth Busted

"In order for my front hall to look good, everything must be put away behind closed doors."

IF YOU HAVE CHILDREN AND NO MUDROOM, consider adding some big bins to your front hall like one of our clients did. Though they lived in a big, beautiful apartment, there wasn't a reasonable place for our client's three sons' tennis bags, backpacks, soccer balls, and all the various items they brought in that were destined to go back out again. Her thought, and it's a good one, is that though she didn't love having a messy front hall, she did love having school-aged sons and was glad they played sports, so she accepted the clutter as part of the joy of being their mother and used the big bins to keep the mayhem contained.

donations. The text method works well with teenagers and college kids even if they're right in the other room. It's wise to let go of expectations of young people joining us in the decluttering with enthusiasm. If it happens, great; but if not, just get their input any way you can.

Gather up everything that had no business being in the front hall to begin with and move it all to the kitchen or to another area of your living space where you won't be tempted to just throw it all back in there. Depending on your home, some items may have to stay in the front hall closet, like tennis rackets (if you truly use them) and cat carriers because if you live in a big city, living the dream might mean having very limited space. For everybody else, don't leave items in the closet that would be better off in the mudroom, garage, basement, or attic.

Umbrellas

Empty out the closet completely and group the items like-with-like. Sort through the subcategories so compact umbrellas are separated from full-size or golf umbrellas. We once pulled forty-six umbrellas from one front hall closet—so don't be too hard on yourself if you find a few all the way in the back that you forgot you had.

> **PRO TIP:**
> # Umbrellas
> Take two umbrellas and put them in your car. They take up almost no space and you'll be so happy to have them should you need them.

Ask yourself how many of those umbrellas have been used in the last year. Is it three? Five? None? Umbrellas gain in numbers because they are often given away at events with company logos, which is how Ann, as a young New Yorker, ended up grabbing one from her umbrella stand and walking down the street, where lots of men smiled at her. It wasn't until she got to her destination and went to close the umbrella that she realized it had the Playboy logo and magazine name across the front.

Simply think about how many you have and how many you can possibly imagine using this year. Like other categories, yes, they sometimes cost money and, yes, they are perfectly good most of the time, but you may live to be a hundred and you won't use the twenty that you currently have (and they will keep coming, anyway), so just let some go. Also consider the space you have for umbrellas. If the bin or stand only holds five, don't keep ten.

No more hunting for your hats or gloves!

Hats, Gloves, and Scarves

Now that you've handled umbrellas, use the same principles to deal with gloves, hats, scarves, and all the other small items. You may need to sort into bins to help you decide how many of each item to keep. If you live with another adult who will be sharing this closet with you, try and keep each person's things in a separate bin. It doesn't help to have all gloves together if you wear different styles and sizes. Each individual needs to know what they have.

There's no reason to keep four pairs of fancy leather gloves if you choose the sporty ones with the texting thumb every single time. Yes, they all cost money and, yes, they are perfectly good; but since you don't use them, they aren't useful to you. The universe is calling, so toss them in the donation bag. (And don't call your mom and ask if she wants them. We've been to her house, too. She has her own glove collection to handle.)

Coats and Jackets

These are big and take up tons of space. They are also expensive guilt producers. They have to be dealt with, or your closet will never function as a place that supports your life and makes it easy to get out of the house—not to mention hanging up the coat of a friend or two.

Can you imagine that ease? Just opening the door and reaching for an empty hanger while your friend picks her jaw up off the floor? She hasn't hung up a friend's coat in a decade either—so this is very impressive. This may have her asking you how in the world you did it—and you may find yourself blabbing about "like-with-like" and "sunk costs."

Keep complementary items close together.

GLOVES
MITTENS

WINTER HATS
MEN

Keep Your Entry Space Running Smoothly

Keep a ladder handy so you can always reach the high shelf.

Often in small spaces, especially workhorse spaces like the front hall closet or mudroom, the trick to keep everything running smoothly is not just organizing methods, but proper storage solutions.

If a redo of the closet isn't possible and you can't reach the only shelf, keep a small stepladder in there (and also in every other room where you can't reach the high shelves of the closets). Stepladders are inexpensive compared to closet renovations, and often provide access to a world of storage that was otherwise a black hole of disorder.

As always, space dictates what you can reasonably keep; but the guiding force should be to make available what you actually wear and use. If all the hats, gloves, and scarves must share one bin in the front hall closet, you'll need to keep less than if you have space for a separate bin for each category in your mudroom.

If you have children and no mudroom, consider making a small area near the front door for them with hooks for jackets and backpacks and a small bench with a basket under it for their shoes.

If you can't reach the shelf above the coats with ease, don't put your things up there. If you live with someone tall who can reach, placing their items up higher makes more sense.

You might consider, for very little money, redoing the interior with an Elfa system from the Container Store. It's easy to design with their help, either in person or online. If you, or your children, can't reach the top shelf, consider installing shelves down one side.

Height Matters

Whenever possible, children should have their own bins and hooks at the appropriate height so they can manage their own things. Autonomy is the goal and the sooner they learn how to handle their own things, the sooner it can be achieved. Also keep in mind that though it may look better to have a lid on a bin, lids make it harder for kids and adults to put things away and find what they're looking for.

Myth Busted

"Everything would be easier if I had a mudroom."

IT MIGHT BE EASIER—but then again it might not be. Big mudrooms where each child has their own cupboard with their name on it are all the rage right now, and they look lovely; but they're not necessary. With the right amount of clothing and gear for each person, and with only the items in your tiny front hall closet that can fit and that belong there, you can make even the smallest space work.

Shelves and Drawers

- **A DRESSER IN THE MUDROOM** or near the front hall closet is so helpful. It can hold sunglasses, sunscreen, keys, hair bands, a brush—and hang a mirror above it so you can take a quick peek before running out the door. You can also use the drawers for gloves and hats.

- **A SET OF TWO ELFA SHELVES FROM THE CONTAINER STORE** in the bottom of the front hall closet uses every inch of space and isn't as fussy as a shoe rack. If you install it about a foot from the floor, the space beneath it can still be used easily—and you've doubled the space for shoes and boots.

This is the place for each person's bin of gloves, hats, etc., and perhaps a bin for the dog's leash and bags. You might even have a space for reusable grocery shopping bags, so you don't forget them anymore.

SENTIMENTAL ITEMS

If you have children, consider putting a Save Forever bin on the shelf in the closet or in the mudroom. The entry space is the place to empty their backpacks—and if there are items that you want to save, you can pop them in the bin. Though drawings or schoolwork may become fridge art first, you still want a bin nearby and not up in your bedroom closet—where so many parents keep their children's Save Forever items.

Owning Well

Invest well and be prepared for any type of weather.

Seasonal Needs

Buy a decent umbrella if you live in a climate where it rains. Everyone thinks they'll lose their umbrella and therefore it's better to buy cheap ones—but if you make Intentional Investments, you'll learn to look after your perfectly functioning umbrella the way you learned to look after your phone. Cheap umbrellas never work well. A nice umbrella is a joy on a rainy day.

Some great Intentional Investments for your entry space are durable bins, strong hooks, and potentially an Elfa system. Keep in mind that these spaces take a lot of abuse from all the comings and goings; look for items that will stand up to all types of weather gear and won't require a lot of upkeep.

Many of the items that end up in entry spaces require end-of-season Mindful Maintenance. Your winter coats may need washing or dry cleaning before they're put away for the warmer months. Check on your boots to see if they need any kind of repairs and then properly store them away until they're needed again.

Your summer gear should be looked after in a similar way. If you invest in nice sandals, they'll need a good cleaning to ensure that they last until next summer. Make sure that your lightweight jackets and sweaters that have been living in the entryway are clean and dry before you store them.

Eco Tips

Your best opportunities to make eco-friendly choices in your entryway spaces start when you walk out the door:

- For your pets, biodegradable dog waste bags are an easy swap. It's not the most pleasant task, but at least you can feel good about making a smart choice in the product you use.

- In the winter, if you live in a cold climate, you can buy pet-friendly ice melt, which is so much nicer for your four-legged family members and any other animals that may walk across your driveway or path.

- In the summer months, nontoxic sunscreens are smart choices. Keep them in a basket by your door and you'll be prepared to walk out the door knowing you're doing your best for your family and the earth.

Keep It Up!

As soon as the front hall closet or the mudroom starts to seem problematic, block out an hour to put it right again. Just like the first time you decluttered, it's a problem of things being there that don't belong there—but this time it will take much less time to fix it. You'll very quickly identify problems, whether an excess of shopping bags or seasonal things like beach bags or skates taking up prime real estate that don't need to be front and center now that the weather has changed. If you do this cleanup whenever it starts to feel crowded or unpleasant, you can zip through the task in very little time.

Gathering
Spaces

Stress-free spaces in which to gather and celebrate

IN SOME HOMES, THE GATHERING SPACE IS one room that functions as a combined living room, dining room, and—because it tends to be more casual and has the television in it—family room. We see this in city apartments all the time. In other homes, these three rooms are separate; though those homes have more square footage, they don't necessarily function any better than the one-room setup.

Our hope for these rooms is for them to be high-functioning spaces that beg to be filled with the friends and family who make life wonderful. All too often, however, these rooms are landing zones for items that belong in other areas of the home. Because people don't know where things belong, many items get dumped in the common areas.

If you don't love these spaces in your home, you may hold back from celebrating life's joyful moments, both big and small. A full family

Thanksgiving dinner, or even pizza with friends, is not a thing you want to take on if you're embarrassed about your space.

You can always go out to meet friends at a restaurant or go to another person's house, but it is wonderful and satisfying to create memories in your own home. Organized gathering spaces make it easier to do so.

Welcoming gathering spaces help create:

Create a space where you can gather and relax.

- **MEANINGFUL CONVERSATIONS** with friends and family
- **SIMPLE JOYS,** like watching a movie together
- **MEMORABLE MEALS**
- **ENJOYABLE DOWNTIME** spent reading a book

Creating Gathering Spaces You Love

Visually unappealing surfaces make these rooms less welcoming and less fun for the adults in the family. It's disheartening to walk into the family room hoping to watch a favorite TV show, only to be confronted by coats and backpacks, piles of toys, mail, and a mound of laundry on the couch.

It is hard to relax when confronted with responsibilities and items on your to-do list, but we can help you fix this. Just think about how you want these rooms to look and feel—and then make it happen. Because gathering rooms are often expensive to change—couches and rugs are expensive—you can start with the work of decluttering and putting simple systems into place, such as a big basket for throws and blankets, and get a new and improved living room for very little money.

How Do You Use Your Gathering Spaces?

Before you begin to organize your gathering spaces, think about the specific spaces you may have and how you want to use them. The three types of spaces—living room, dining room, and family room—tend to work in sync.

- **DO YOU LIVE ALONE OR WITH OTHERS?**
- **IF YOU HAVE KIDS, HOW OLD ARE THEY?**
- **DO YOU LIKE TO ENTERTAIN?** When you do, is it a more formal dinner party or ordering pizza and watching the game?
- **IF YOU HAVE A DINING ROOM,** is it used as such? Or is it a room that is mostly empty? Could the space be used for something that would better serve your family?

- **DO YOU HAVE ALL THREE OF THESE SPACES**—living room, dining room, and family room? Or do you have a room that is less formal than a designated living room and is more like a family room but with a table in the corner so it also works as the dining room?

Questions like these help you to understand your space. If you rarely, if ever, have a formal dinner party but you have a set of china for twelve taking up space in the prime real estate of your home, you might want to ask yourself why. Sometimes we feel we are supposed to have or do certain things. When we realize they don't serve our current life, it's much easier to let go.

The truth about these rooms is they often lack storage or spaces to tuck belongings away so, though we want them to look good all the time, they seldom do. The fastest way to achieve gathering spaces you love is to make sure there is nothing in these rooms that doesn't need to be there. Once the excess is gone, you'll be able to see if you need to add in a couple of new pillows on the couch to make things look more welcoming and more pleasing. To make tidying up easier, you may want to consider adding furniture that allows you to put things away, such as an ottoman that opens for storage.

SORT AND DECIDE

Reducing the items in each of these categories will result in a living space you are proud of.

Books

Generally speaking, you're a book lover or you're not. If not, you can skip along to the next section. If you are, your bookshelves are likely an area that could use some work. Books definitely fall into the category of things that multiply—and now that browsing in the local bookshop is just one way to buy books, you may find that Amazon is helping the multiplication process along. If you are a book lover but your spouse is not, the bookshelves can become an area of contention—not to mention the stacks on the floor and the bedside tables. Curating your books is a lifelong commitment, and you may find that it is fun and satisfying to have only what you truly love looking back at you from your shelves.

The trick is to take all the books off the shelves and put them in stacks around your chair or on a table. You don't have to empty the entire book area all at one time; you can go shelf by shelf in case you tire of the project —but do empty each shelf that you're working on completely. Hold each

Sure, books and movies are great, but are they all worth saving?

Keep only what you really want
and will actually read…or reread.

book and read the dust jacket or cover. Will you read it again? Is this one an old friend that reminds you of a certain time in your life, and without it your house wouldn't feel like home? If you aren't deeply attached, let it go. You don't have to keep any book just because you feel you should. A person can have a complete life and an interesting collection of books without *Moby-Dick* or *Sense and Sensibility*; but if *you* can't, then by all means pop those two back on the shelves.

Like every other area of your home, the goal is to keep only what you use, love, or want. You want your shelves to make you happy when you look at them. Bookshelves can become emotionally weighty if they're full of books you feel you should read, or books you've kept that were gifts but which you have no interest in reading. Let them all go.

When the ones that remain are all books you truly want, it's time to decide how to style your shelves. We organize books by category. We tried color coding the books in our office—it lasted for about a year—and then after we got tired of not being able to quickly find what we were looking for, we took them all out, put them back in subcategories, and guess what? We also got rid of a lot when we pulled them off of the shelves to redo them.

Get those blankets off the floor!

Candles

Gather all the candles in one area. This is a simple exercise because you probably know exactly which ones you like and which ones will never be used (maybe they were gifts and/or you don't like the scent). Release those to the universe. It's better not to put candles in the donate bag because they can melt and make a mess; but if there's room you can add them to a box of kitchen items being donated. If they've been used at all (if the wick has been lit even once), they are garbage.

Throws and Blankets

Bet you didn't think you'd have that *Frozen* blanket on your couch eight years later! They don't call it a family room for nothing—so even though you

envision a beautiful room that looks like a Pottery Barn catalog, this is what you've got. That squishy pillow your special someone uses for his back while playing video games and the cartoon blankets that are most definitely not made from natural materials are here to stay. Don't fight it. It's a stage (even if it's a long one). Years from now, you'll take the *Frozen* blanket off the shelf and ask your daughter if she wants to take it to her new apartment. She'll look at you like you're crazy—and only you will remember that you sacrificed your personal aesthetics for her comfort. But she will go forward into the world as a young woman who was loved, whose taste and needs were respected, and who felt cozy in the family room. What a lucky girl.

Toys and Games

We have seen so many living rooms and family rooms that are buried under toys. Many of our clients are dismayed that their children have so much, because they grew up in a time when children had less. But the adults have a lot to do with the problem. This is in no way a criticism of the parents. From what we've seen in our lives, and the lives and homes of our clients, parenthood means resisting a nearly endless tsunami of toys.

Everywhere children go they see things they want, and so much of it is inexpensive—and also fun and interesting. A parent can say no 90 percent of the time . . . and still that's a lot of $2 Matchbox cars making their way home from the grocery store (not to mention holiday and birthday gifts, the zoo, museums, or theme parks). You're truly only safe at the park or the library. So, what to do?

You can work with your older children to solve this problem—and stay on top of it, so you're only decluttering in 15- to 30-minute blocks of time. Children don't have the interest or the attention span to spend an afternoon going through all their belongings. It doesn't make them bad; it just makes them kids. They can likely make five to ten decisions, depending on their age, before they lose interest.

The best approach is to take a crack at it yourself: Gather all the actual garbage together so you can show them what is being tossed and explain why (broken, missing piece, etc.). Don't keep toys they tell you they don't want, no matter who gave them to your child or what they cost. If you

STOP STEPPING ON LEGOS!
Rein in the chaos with a
well-curated play area.

Bins and baskets make playtime and cleanup a breeze!

think it's something they may grow into, then put it up on a closet shelf and try again in six months. But generally, just like adults, kids know what they like and dislike.

When working with children, consider doing a category a day. For example, get all the dinosaurs together and ask if the two broken ones can go. Sometimes the child will tell you they don't like dinosaurs anymore—which you won't believe because it was such a huge thing for so long. He's likely telling you the truth, but because the dinosaur collection cost a small fortune, you should box them up and put them in the garage for now. If he never revisits this earlier obsession, you'll be the awesome aunt or neighbor when other children come to visit.

Keep Your Gathering Spaces Running Smoothly

As much as these spaces require organizing, they also require good design so that things can be hidden away when not in use. Storage solutions and functional furniture can help to keep these spaces clutter free:

- **IF YOU DON'T HAVE BUILT-IN SHELVES OR CABINETS** in your living room or family room areas, consider purchasing a piece of furniture for storage. You can use bins to organize toys or games.
- **YOU CAN ALSO PURCHASE AN IKEA KALLAX SHELVING UNIT** or find a used one on Facebook Marketplace. They come in all different sizes and configurations. You can purchase bins that fit inside the cube shelves and are big enough to hold all sorts of things.
- **BINS UNDER YOUR COFFEE TABLE** are a great place for the *Frozen* blanket or for toys.
- **THERE'S AN EXPRESSION IN** the resale/estate cleanout business: "Brown is down." This means the brown furniture that people purchased for decades isn't worth much . . . but it also means it doesn't cost much. If

Look for furniture that does double duty.

you're at all handy and have the space to paint furniture, you can watch zillions of YouTube videos that will show you how to do it. You can pick up well-made brown furniture for a song and then sand and repaint it and turn it into something amazing.

Because these rooms are used by all family members, the systems should be clear and easy for everyone to follow. For example, a bin for throws and blankets is much easier for teenagers to manage than a display blanket ladder. Asking your teenagers to fold and arrange blankets on a ladder is likely to lead to disappointment, but if your teens do it, post a photo of the miracle and see if it goes viral.

The same goes for little children and their toys. Having bins for broad categories of toys (e.g., "cars") makes it easier for them to help with cleaning up. Your child cannot put board games back in color-coded order on high shelves—but they can stack them up inside the ottoman with the lift-up top.

SENTIMENTAL ITEMS

While considering what you might need to make your gathering spaces work well for you, for your family, and for how you live now, also ask yourself what pieces of furniture can go. You might not think of furniture as clutter—but it can be, especially when it no longer works in your home. Furniture often falls into the category of "It costs so much money"; usually when you buy a chair, a table, or a storage piece, you purchase the best you can afford at that time. Young people may receive furniture from relatives when they are just starting out and simply need somewhere to sit and eat. If this was you, you were probably grateful then; but that old table may not fit in your dining nook, or

Display a couple pictures you love instead of a bunch you just like.

Do you use this old set of china or is it just gathering dust?

you've never used all eight chairs at once (if you only ever use six, get rid of the other two). This can be hard because it's a set; what if I have a party; I don't want to hurt Aunt Mary's feelings even though she's no longer with us; and a million other reasons we might want to keep things. But there is also reality. Items that are not used are clutter.

Myth Busted

"You must use your dining room as a dining room."

WE HAD A CLIENT WHO DID A LOVELY RENOVATION OF HER KITCHEN. It completely reflected how she and her family lived. They ate all their meals at the kitchen table. She decided not to knock down the wall and absorb the space of the dining room into the new kitchen because she had inherited her grandmother's table and chairs and felt she had to keep the set—maybe forever. The saddest part was, she didn't even like the set. Her grandmother had been gone for many years; but she didn't want to hurt her mother by getting rid of *her* mother's table and chairs.

We suggested she call her mom and ask her if she had any feelings about it. Turns out our client's mom didn't care if her daughter kept it because she never liked the set anyway! She thought her daughter loved it because she'd dragged it from house to house since inheriting it.

Our client was relieved; she decided to turn the dining room into a lounge and homework area for the kids. This way they were able to work and relax nearby while she got dinner started in the kitchen. Her only complaint was that she hadn't done it sooner—it would have been a perfect playroom when her kids were little.

Owning Well

Create a space that serves the life you have now.

Make Choices for Life Stages

Purchases for gathering spaces tend to be pricey and should be made carefully, as Intentional Investments. Is a leather sectional that seats an entire eighth-grade basketball team really necessary? Or, at this stage of your life, would a microsuede couch and some beanbags be a better fit? Ask yourself what kinds of furniture suit your current lifestyle and buy accordingly. If you're at a point where you can maintain a more formal, sophisticated look, do your research and get something fantastic that will last for many years.

The theory of **Owning Well** is to buy the best you can afford and take care of it—though this may not apply to the couch in your family room if you have children and pets. Your money may be better spent on a more affordable couch with fabric that is likelier to come clean and also last for years.

Once you've decided on the types of furniture best suited to your gathering spaces, take care of them with Mindful Maintenance! It doesn't matter if you decided to purchase the inexpensive couch that your kids can relax on, you still want it to last and look decent. Mindful Maintenance is about keeping your items in good shape for as long as possible, regardless of the purchase price.

If you own silver, you likely don't use it as often as you (or your parents) once did. If you do want to use it once in a while, make sure to cover it in plastic wrap after you polish it. It's so wonderful to go get it to set the table and find it as shiny as it was when you put it away.

Eco Tips

Our best eco tip for gathering spaces goes hand in hand with Mindful Maintenance. Furniture of all kinds ends up in landfills and, as you can imagine, takes up a ton of space. If you can take good care of your couches, tables, lamps, and other large objects, you can donate them when you decide to upgrade. Goodwill, Habitat for Humanity, and other charitable organizations will make sure that your gently used but still serviceable items go to a good home.

Keep It Up!

A monthly decluttering of the gathering spaces, where you simply remove the things that don't belong in the living room, family room, or dining room but somehow ended up there, is enough to keep these rooms running smoothly for years to come. Done every month, this should never take more than an hour and will often take less.

Laundry, Linens, Cleaning, and Utility

Spaces that make managing your home efficient and easy

LIKE MAKING MEALS, LAUNDRY AND CLEANING are things most of us do many times a week. A room, or space, that is set up to be as functional as possible makes these chores more manageable.

Most laundry rooms in a house either have lots of things that don't need to be there but somehow ended up there; or the laundry room was the only reasonable space to stash things and, though not perfect, it's the best choice.

After you organize the space, many of these items will stay in the laundry room if you live in a smaller home; while in a bigger house they may be moved to separate spaces and closets.

We'll tackle linens, cleaning supplies, pet supplies, and utility items in this section—but if you store those objects somewhere other than the laundry room, similar rules will apply.

It's important to make purposeful choices not only about which room the items belong in, but also where in the laundry room the items should go. Good decisions will help this space function efficiently.

An organized laundry room matters. It can help you:

- **SAVE TIME** on everyday tasks
- **MAKE IT EASY** to tackle a laundry mountain
- **REDUCE STRESS** around over-purchasing and wasting money
- **ENJOY THE FEELING** that comes from a handling a task that previously felt impossible

PRO TIP:

Laundromats and Other Shared Laundry Spaces

If you live in an apartment building with a shared laundry room, or if you take your laundry out, return your laundry card to a designated spot and keep your detergent in a closet by the front door so you can easily grab it on your way to do laundry. Also consider getting a laundry bag with backpack straps. It's an absolute game changer if you have far to walk.

Creating a Laundry Room You Love

The size of your laundry "room" dictates how it can be used. Sometimes it's just a closet that fits a stackable washer and dryer; sometimes it's a large and somewhat luxurious place you wouldn't mind escaping to multiple times a day.

Be honest with yourself about how you like to do your folding, because that will dictate how you use your space. Some people haul it all out to fold while watching TV; others do it in the laundry room.

If there's room for a table, that's a great addition to any laundry room. Make sure it's high enough that your back is straight while you're folding. You will literally spend hours of your life here so don't mess around. Some people have the washer and dryer next to each other and can fold on top of the machines; this works too, though not quite as well.

Your laundry room could be not only functional but pleasant too.

How Do You Use Your Laundry Room?

As elsewhere in your home, items end up in laundry rooms that don't belong there. Now is the time to get rid of the excess. The objective is to make this room less irritating than it currently is, so ask yourself the following questions:

- **WHAT IS STORED IN YOUR LAUNDRY ROOM CURRENTLY?** Go there and really take a look.
- **WHICH OF THESE ITEMS NEED TO STAY HERE?** Besides laundry detergent and fabric softener, you are making a choice to keep the other items there.
- **WHERE DO YOU LIKE TO FOLD YOUR LAUNDRY?**
- **WHERE DO PEOPLE IN YOUR HOUSEHOLD LOOK FOR THINGS** such as cleaning supplies, batteries, and pet supplies?

Thinking clearly about how you really live and use your space will help you set your laundry room up for maximum efficiency.

SORT AND DIVIDE

Some of these categories include multiple items. Subcategorizing will allow you to see what's working for you and what's working against you.

Sheets and Towels

In order to sort sheets for decluttering, they should be subdivided into piles of twins, queens, kings, pillowcases, random bed skirts, mattress pads—all of it. Within each group there are some that really should just go. You spend a third of your one precious life in bed. Don't let it be on stained, torn, or yellowed sheets. You can't control everything in life; mostly you can't control anything. But, you have the ability to make such a nice bed for yourself without spending a fortune. Then at the end of each day, when life has thrown all sorts of crazy at you, you just slip

Don't just shove your linens in the closet! Sort 'em by type and size.

into your perfect bed and say "Aahhh" and know that you're worth this bit of bliss.

What is the right number of sheets? For the adult bed, two full sets with a whole extra set of pillowcases works well. If you have a king-size bed with six pillows, that means you need two flat sheets, two fitted sheets, and eighteen pillowcases. The cases wear out faster than the sheets, so rotate them more frequently and they will last as long as the rest of the set. For children's beds, follow the same rule—with one or two extra bottom sheets for the children's beds if they're still at an age where accidents can happen.

Towels should be subdivided by larger bath sheets, regular-size towels, hand towels, washcloths, and beach towels. People tend to keep old towels for rags and to use with pets. That's OK—but be realistic about how many rags you need to "wash the car" when you in fact go to the car wash every time. We also know the more towels you have, the more towels your children (and maybe even you, you criminal) will use. That means more laundry.

We recommend having no more than three bath towels per person. Most people have far more than this—hence the packed linen closet. Everyone uses all the space they have and most people continue to buy until no more fits. **You don't have to live like this. You can truly only have exactly what you need.** And if you're worried you won't have enough towels, get some Turbie Twist hair towels for the people with long hair. They're effective and take up little space.

How many beach towels do you need? Only enough for the entire family to go to the pool or the beach together. Five people in your family? Five beach towels plus two for guests. Seven beach towels take up so much less space than twenty.

If you have a pool at your house, it's a different question: How much laundry do you feel like doing every day, all summer? The more towels you have, the more your friends and family will use. Every day. All summer. Every summer. Forever. These are the laws of nature. If you want to do less laundry, supply fewer towels.

Table Linens

Ann recently hosted a large group for Christmas Eve. Because her guests couldn't fit at her dining table, she bought a large catering table, knowing it would be used again and again. The table was so large she didn't have a big enough tablecloth to put on it, but because the table wasn't attractive in any way, she wanted it to be covered all the way to the floor. Ann clicked away on Amazon and the next day a white polyester number was delivered. While setting the table, the inexpensive cloth went on first with one of her beautiful linen tablecloths on top of it. On Christmas Eve, red wine was spilled—of course red wine was spilled! That's what happens at parties! Later that night, after the guests were gone, Ann soaked both tablecloths. The wine came right out of the linen cloth that had come from her grandmother's linen collection but wouldn't budge from the

KING SETS

QUEEN SETS

QUEEN DUVET

FULL DUVET

TWIN DUVET

TWIN SETS

KING CASES

STANDARD CASES

STANDARD SHAMS

BATH MAT

TWIN MATTRESS PAD

*Keep only
what you need,
use, and want
to wash!*

polyester cloth. That one went into the trash. Trying to save money, Ann had simply wasted it.

Which brings us to handling linens—both purchasing and storing them. Don't cheap out if you can possibly avoid it. Inexpensive cloth doesn't work very well. Cheap towels don't absorb, and they fray. Cheap sheets pill and stain. Inexpensive items aren't inexpensive when you have to buy them over and over, year after year. If you get the higher-quality item, you will spend more when you buy but spend less over the years.

Because the generation that is downsizing often had nice-quality table linens, consider buying those at a vintage store. We have sent tons of them to be donated on behalf of our clients.

A final word about linen closets—if you choose quality items and don't over-purchase, you'll save money as well as time and aggravation. You and your family won't have enough towels to keep grabbing fresh ones every day, which means you'll save on doing laundry and therefore using less water and less detergent. You'll have less to fold. And not just towels that are sort of fun to fold because let's admit it, in a life full of chores, it's sort of satisfying to place those nice rectangles on top of each other until you have a big stack of towels. You'll also fold fewer fitted sheets and seriously, who understands how that woman on YouTube does that trick anyway?

Don't pretend you don't know what we're talking about. She has twenty-two million views.

Sentimental Linens

Would you believe most people hold on to linens for sentimental reasons? I think you would. It can be children's crib sheets, or an old set of sheets that are super soft . . . but also ratty looking, so they'll never be used again. It can be the first "good" sheets someone ever bought, or towels from their grandparents' beach house. Well-made linens last and last; but if nobody is using them they are essentially clutter—big clutter, because they take up so much space. A quilt that Grandma made but nobody uses is a problem.

We have a sister/aunt who is an amazing quilter and the idea of tossing one of her quilts in the donate bag is obscene to us—but if it isn't being used, at least move it up to the highest shelf and out of the way of everyday life. This is more or less what happens in most linen closets—high up and way back is where the unused items go—but it's often thoughtless and the "system" hasn't been updated in years . . . so, as in every other room, take it all out and start sorting.

It's tempting to keep more than you need in the linen closet. Maybe because nature abhors a vacuum? We'll leave that to the physicists. But we will say this: Only once have we seen an empty drawer—and we've never seen an empty closet. Think about that. We're in people's homes every single day.

Detergents and Other Supplies

Cleaning products are one of those groups where new things come in but nothing ever leaves. It takes a long time to finish products that aren't used regularly, or at all, and yet we all keep buying. You might find something you like better, because it's greener or has a different scent or is organic. Sometimes you find the organic glass cleaner doesn't work as well as Windex and so you go back to the Windex. That's OK. Don't beat yourself up about it. Mistakes have been made. Just don't keep the ones that you no longer use.

We don't know why we all keep buying; we just do. Maybe we're all susceptible to the marketing and branding that companies spend so much money on, or maybe life becomes routine and we just want to mix it up a little so we buy the new hand soap. Look at us, living on the edge!

So, your job now is to sort the cleaning supplies the same way you would anything else. Pull them all out, group like-with-like, and use subcategories to see what you actually have. Once you've separated them all into categories such as

Be honest and toss the cleaners that aren't working for you.

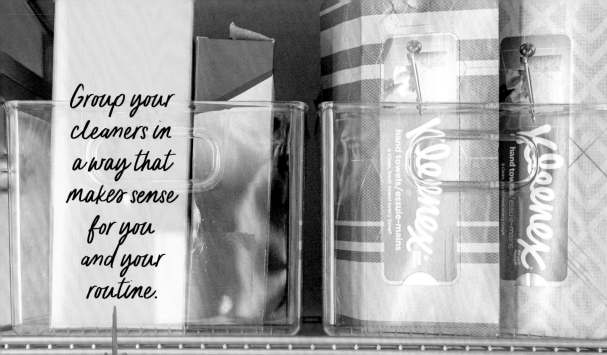

Group your cleaners in a way that makes sense for you and your routine.

detergents, soaps, Windex-like products, floor cleaners, toilet cleaners, and specialty polishes (like silver and copper), take a first pass and get rid of all the strange, unused things that just didn't work out for one reason or another.

Take another pass and get rid of all the things that are no longer in use, like the supplies for dog messes that you no longer use because your sweet pup died five years ago. Don't slow down to judge yourself and think about the wasted money. It's done now. Save the scolding, interior monologue for the cleaning products aisle at the store. You can save a fortune by not buying what you don't need. You'll get 100 percent off!

Once it is all sorted, put it back in a way that makes sense for you and prevents mistakes in the future. For Ann, that means keeping it to one bin that takes up half the space under the kitchen sink—she has only what can fit in there. That being said, her home isn't large and if she had a few more bathrooms upstairs, she might have another set of supplies up there.

One last thing: If you're going to keep your most frequently used cleaning products like toilet paper, paper towels, and other backstock from Costco in the laundry room, make space for those items. If you don't have a cabinet that can hold twenty rolls of paper towels, they will, of course, end up on the floor. In our honest opinion, bulk shopping is a disaster when it comes to smaller homes and apartments. We recommend buying what you can use within a few weeks.

As always, take the time to figure out how much money you're saving and then factor in what it's costing you, stress-wise. You're reading this manifesto on organizing your home because it's as challenging for you as it is for most of us. Too much stuff in too small a space is the major problem when it comes to easy, efficient home management. That's it. Lecture is over.

Utility Storage

Utility areas are just like junk drawers. They are often a disaster when they should be a high-functioning area that supports the home. Due to the layout of modern homes, people often keep all utility items either in a cabinet in the laundry room or a small closet in the home. Either way, the rules remain the same.

Utility areas contain:

- Light bulbs
- Batteries
- Tools
- Craft/hobbies/gardening
- Manuals/directions
- Tape of all sorts
- Shoe polish

Keep your batteries in one place so you can find them!

We often find so much space in large utility closets after decluttering that we're able to use them for our Instagram photos! Imagine that!

In order to make your utility closet work as well as possible, first declutter in the way we've taught you. Take every single thing out. Sort into categories and subcategories. Once everything is in like-with-like piles, gather up items you don't want, need, like, or use and place them in garbage bags or donation bags, depending on whether or not the items could be useful to somebody else.

Even in utility closets, we don't recommend having a backstock of very many things. For the most part, people forget what they've purchased. Unless their home is perfectly organized, there is overbuying and waste. Light bulbs and batteries are exceptions that prove the rule—these can both be purchased in bulk. It's aggravating to have to go out and get those at the moment you need them, and since they don't wear out quickly, you won't end up throwing them away and wasting money. (Yes, yes—batteries do get funky and leak when they're super old but that isn't going to happen to you again. Your home will be too organized for that!)

When setting up your utility closet, take a minute to ask yourself not only *what* is going to go in there but *who* will be taking things out. If you have children who are old enough to get batteries, light bulbs, and flashlights themselves but are not tall enough to reach the top shelves, place those items on lower shelves.

Some back-up
items are good,
but keep them
within reason.

BATTERIES

EXTENSION
CORDS

BICYCLE
GEAR

TOOLS

DRILLS

GARDEN GEAR

Even narrow storage like this can create order and ease in an otherwise busy space.

One of the most important things we've learned from our many clients who are mothers is that whether or not they work outside of the home, they are still doing a larger percentage of the housework than anybody else in their family. We have heard from many of them that after Done & Done Home sorted out and organized their entire homes, it was easier for them to get things done themselves, of course, but it was also easier to push their children toward doing things for themselves.

Keep Your Laundry Room Running Smoothly

As with all other areas of the home, keeping items in their sections will help make your laundry room organized, but since it is a space that often holds items from multiple categories, we suggest more bins and labeling than we would in typical spaces.

Since you now have all your light bulbs, cleaning supplies, and linens decluttered and sectioned, we suggest that you keep those groups together (whether that's in a cabinet, bin, drawer, or closet) and label things clearly so that everyone in the house knows where to find something, but more importantly where to put it back.

How you handle your laundry and your family's laundry will depend somewhat on personal preference. Some people prefer to do frequent small loads, while apartment dwellers might save it up and do several loads all at once in the shared laundry room with multiple washers and dryers.

Whatever you decide, it's easier if you have a system and everyone in your household understands their part in it.

Laundry and Children

If you have a laundry room, decanting your supplies can make things even more enjoyable—just make sure they're out of very young children's reach.

We've learned a few tricks from some of our clients when it comes to dealing with young people and the laundry:

Assign each kid their own towel pattern or color.

1 **GIVE EACH CHILD A TOWEL THAT IS A SEPARATE COLOR** that is always theirs, so they only use that one; and only give them one towel a week. If one of your children has long hair, get them a Turbie Twist hair towel, and encourage them to let it dry out afterward because if left in a ball in their room, it will stink. Explain once why it stinks and then leave them to it.

2 **TEACH YOUR OLDER CHILDREN TO DO THEIR OWN LAUNDRY** when they're young enough to think it's cool and grown-up to use the machines. From what we've seen, children as young as eight, depending on the child, can easily handle it.

3 **DON'T COMMENT ON THEIR CRAZY FOLDING.** They'll get the hang of it after a couple of years and, more important, you don't have to do it.

4 **PURGE YOUR CHILDREN'S CLOTHES** so that they only have exactly what they need and wear in their dressers and closets. Running out of clean clothes is good for them—especially when they do their own laundry.

PRO TIP:
Pet Supplies

It's not a bad idea to keep backstock items for pets in the laundry room or in a utility closet, but most of the things we need for our pets on a daily basis—food, litter, leashes, and brushes—are best kept right near where we use them.

Myth Busted

"Buying things on sale is always a good idea!"

SALE ITEMS ARE FINE IF IT'S SOMETHING YOU ALREADY BUY and you're low on stock—but usually sales work better for the seller than the buyer. The seller is trying to get rid of things that didn't sell during the season, so unless you've had your eye on something and watched the price come down all season long, you're likely to be buying something you don't truly need.

Take a deep breath before purchasing sale items and ask yourself why you're really buying something—to own the particular item, or just to save 30 percent on "something"?

Owning Well

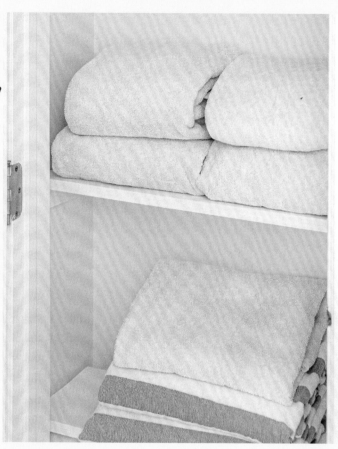

Storing and cleaning your items with care will help them last longer.

Choosing Linens and Other Fabrics

As we discussed above, good-quality linens have the potential to last for generations. We recommend making Intentional Investments. However, if you have a kids' table at Thanksgiving, then you know, without a doubt, that food and drinks are going to get spilled. In this case, perhaps the festive, inexpensive tablecloth is the better option.

Another example is our client who has four dogs who sleep in her bed. Would her money be well spent if she bought expensive, high-quality sheets? Not a chance. She replaces her sheets several times a year; and for her, the best option is the cheaper one.

It's good to remember that an Intentional Investment is not always the most expensive thing you can find. It's about thinking about your purchases before you make them so that your home runs as efficiently as possible.

As we discussed in the bedroom section, a great hack for keeping your workout clothes smelling fresh is to add a capful of Head & Shoulders shampoo to your wash. Guess what? It works for towels too! No matter how often you wash those bath towels, sooner or later they tend to get that musty smell. Keep your towels lasting longer with this simple trick. That's Mindful Maintenance!

Eco Tips

A multitude of eco-friendly laundry products are available that will reduce the toxins in your wash water and have packaging that is recyclable and responsible. You can also choose wool balls over dryer sheets for your dryer; and washing in cold water is also a great option.

Keep It Up!

Your laundry room will stay pretty well organized if each grouping (sheets, towels, cleaning supplies, light bulbs, etc.) has the correct amount in it and the items are contained and well labeled. If you feel things are getting tight, over-purchasing is usually the culprit. Take a quick look at the cleaning supplies because that's an area where the mystery of multiplication happens. Be decisive about what isn't working and toss those items now. The better organized your laundry room is, the less often you'll be wasting money on cleaning supplies that you don't need.

Children's Spaces

Bedrooms and playrooms for children that foster
creativity, independence, and easy cleanup

PLAYROOMS AND CHILDREN'S BEDROOMS SHOULD BE spaces where
children can have fun and enjoy themselves. They should be easy for
parents to manage. When children have the correct amount of toys and
clothes for their space and age, it is easier for them to find what they
want to play with and to choose what they want to wear. Putting everything back at the end of the day becomes possible.

In our work, we see playrooms packed full of toys. Children's and
teens' bedrooms are also full of things—on shelves, in cubbies and
bins, in under-the-bed drawers, and piled in corners around the room.
Closets are packed, and so are dressers—not just inside but on top. This
clutter makes it hard for kids to play—let alone be independent and help
with things like cleaning up and putting laundry away.

As parents, you're playing the long game—this isn't just about a tidy room today. It's about raising a child to become an adult who can function in their own home.

A room with only belongings a child uses and loves is incredibly helpful to both kids and parents:

A great play space works for you and your kids.

- **IT MAKES IT EASIER FOR CHILDREN** to handle their own belongings.
- **IT REDUCES STRESS FOR PARENTS**—because raising children is hard enough without fighting about messy clutter.
- **RESEARCH SHOWS THAT CHILDREN ARE HAPPIER** when they aren't over-whelmed by choices.
- **KIDS WILL HAVE AN EASIER TIME** taking care of their things when they have fewer possessions to deal with.

Remember—this phase does pass. One day, you'll walk past their bedroom and there won't be any large, plastic, bright-colored toys left in there. Her laptop will be on her desk; his phone will be on the charger. The mess will be gone, though so will the magic of having young children at home—so, for now, when you're in the middle of toy hell, be patient with them and with yourself. Do your best not to overconsume and be relaxed about the gifts that come into your home from friends and family. If it's not right for your child, or you have too much currently, put it up on a designated shelf for regifting, or for a day down the line when your child is looking for something to do.

How Do Your Children Use Their Spaces?

Let's find out how your children use their space in your home so we can make the most of it:

- **DO YOUR KIDS HAVE A PLAYROOM** and a bedroom each, or is everything in the bedroom?
- **DO YOU HAVE A BUSY, ACTIVE CHILD** or a peaceful, quiet child? All children are a little of both, of course, but how high-energy are your kids?
- **WHAT DOES YOUR CHILD MAINLY LIKE TO DO AT HOME?** Crafts? Reading? Destroy your living room?
- **WHO IS SENTIMENTAL ABOUT THE THINGS THE CHILD HAS OUTGROWN?** You or your child?
- **DOES THE CHILD HAVE ANY INTEREST IN PUTTING THINGS AWAY,** or is it always a fight?

Thinking through these questions will help you to establish good systems for your kids to pitch in and help care for your home. And who doesn't want more help?

Does your family read all these books or are they just taking up space?

SORT AND DECIDE

Help your child work through letting go of things—systems for decluttering with children are different than when you are decluttering alone or helping other adults. Like-with-like works particularly well with children. They might not give the OK for an individual car or dress-up outfit to go, but when their toys are all together and they start to pick their favorites—what we call "definitely keep" when working with adults—kids learn there are also things they don't care about as much anymore.

The Trouble with Toys

Eliminating extra toys is tough for a variety of reasons:

1 **SOFT TOYS WILL NOT BE ACCEPTED AT DONATION CENTERS** because of the fear of bedbugs.

2 **TOYS THAT ARE MISSING PIECES ARE NOT WANTED.**

3 **TOYS THAT ARE UNOPENED CAN BE DONATED**—but many people remain hopeful that the unopened toys will be used and want to hold on to them too.

4 **MANY FAMILIES HANG ON TO TOYS** because they don't know how many children they'll have and don't want to rebuy them in the future.

5 **SOMETIMES PARENTS ARE SIMPLY ATTACHED TO TOYS** that their children were attached to, even though the child remembers nothing about it.

All of this makes emotional and practical sense—but the basic conflict still exists. Where is it all going to be stored?

We try our hardest—Kate as a mother, and Ann as a grandmother—to be careful about buying toys for Kate's children. Sometimes we succeed and sometimes we don't. Kate does succeed in donating things as soon as they are outgrown, so long as the toys are in good shape and she knows other children would be delighted to have them. If the toys are broken or missing parts, they are garbage. It's good to keep this in mind when buying cheap things that won't last through even one child, let alone two. Yes, good toys are more expensive; but if they can be passed from child to child, then the cost per use—and the cost to the environment—is more reasonable.

Kate has had relative success sorting toys the way she sorts the boys' clothes—every few months she gathers the toys together and declutters, knowing that anything James has outgrown *can* be saved for Charlie—but first she asks herself if it *should* be saved. She has bins marked by age in the attic; but with a three-and-a-half-year difference between the boys, that's a lot of toys and clothes. There is also the reality that Charlie may not want to play with the same sorts of toys that James likes (and Charlie will also receive his own Christmas and birthday presents).

The truth is, it can't all stay forever. Do your best to buy as little as possible, and sort and donate often. Also remember that this stage of their lives will end in time, and eventually you'll likely only have a few toys up on a shelf in a closet or one bin in the attic. As with so many things related to parenting, in the future your life will be easier in some ways and harder in others. You may look back and wonder how a toy-filled living room was the thing that stressed you out the most.

With this in mind, let's go through the rest of the children's belongings:

Puzzles make great gifts, but if your kids aren't into them, let them go.

Board Games and Puzzles

The strange thing is that most of the games and toys don't seem to get much use. Kids, like the rest of us, want tech. We all have more to entertain us than ever before, but we use way less because our phones, computers, and iPads are the standard go-to for fun. Parents do all they can to limit screen time—maybe that's one of the reasons there is such an excess of other toys.

For our clients and for ourselves, board games and puzzles are another area where fantasy and reality collide. Family game night looms large in the minds of parents with middle-school-age kids—but, in reality, it's very hard to pull off. The rainy-day puzzle-doing does happen but how often; and once the two-thousand-piece puzzle is done, do they want to do it again? Think

How many of these games have you truly played more than once?

about how often game night actually happens; two nights a year is not enough to justify twenty board games in the closet. Try reducing the board games by half. Better yet, schedule a game night and see which ones are still popular with your family. Keep those.

Create an art area that can grow with your kids and will keep the chaos to a minimum.

Art and Crafting Supplies

This collection of things grows like mad even when you're constantly sorting and cleaning it. The magic of multiplication means paper, glitter, glue, stickers, yarn, paints, and slime will all keep coming. Just do your best. It helps to have a designated area that can't grow, such as a cabinet or a set of shelves with bins on it. Some children simply love making stuff, and if it helps keep them off their screens, that's a win even if it's a mess.

LEGO

From what we've seen, the kids who like to build things out of random LEGO pieces are less common by far than the ones who want to build the Eiffel Tower and the Pirate Ship. Some kids would rather use their imaginations to create original things, but in our experience, both on the job and in our own homes, most kids want to build those big dust collectors and then never play with them again. That doesn't mean they want to get rid of them. We've seen bedrooms that were designed to display all the built LEGO sets. We've moved so much LEGO that we even have an expression for what can happen if we don't wrap sections in tight plastic wrap. It's called "LEGO Tears"—which refers to the frustration a young person feels after spending hours and hours of their life building something, only to have it broken during a move. One summer a few years ago, we moved so many families with so much LEGO, we almost hired a teenager to put it all back together in the new homes.

The clever folks at LEGO understand us. They design things that delight and amaze us.

But what happens next? Yes, some LEGO is recycled, and some can be sold or sent in for donation. But the truth is, it's very hard to get rid of. It's as if we built a jigsaw puzzle and expected it to stay on the dining room table forever. The Sydney Opera House designed by LEGO is way cooler than a standard jigsaw puzzle and takes more time to complete. It also costs more money. If you got only one big LEGO set a year for your child, starting at age six or seven, and gave one every year until college, you'd have twelve or so big projects. Perhaps you're chuckling at the idea of college kids getting LEGO for a gift. If so, you haven't seen the recently released Central Perk from *Friends*.

We've helped families where all the LEGO boxes and direction booklets were saved in the hopes of dismantling them at some point and packing them up so they could be rebuilt later. We've helped families that had massive bins of pieces but no directions because, "They're online." We've helped families that

For goodness' sake, how much LEGO do you really need?

PRO TIP:
Tidy Toys

Only store toys in the living room that can be neatly contained and tidy. Yes to Duplo, cars, Magna-Tiles, and dolls. No to glitter, Play-Doh, or markers.

did repack them all perfectly and hoped to "save them for their grandchildren."

Kate is trying to teach James from an early age that once they build the LEGO set, they can enjoy it for a few days or a week and then she puts it back in the box with the instructions for another day. So far, so good. But he's only five and she knows it's much easier for him to accept dismantling a 200-piece car that they built in a few hours than it will be to dismantle the 5,900-piece Taj Mahal.

You'll have to figure out what works for your family. If you have the space, there is no harm in storing the LEGO whether they are built or taken apart. But if your child is done with LEGO, perhaps you know of another child who might like to have them.

Clothing and Shoes

A great habit to get into anytime your child tries on clothing that doesn't fit anymore or they don't want to wear—much like in your adult closet—is to teach them to put it in a donate or hand-me-down bin in their closet. As best as you can, try not to question their choices. Maybe they aren't sentimental (and you are), or perhaps they don't like the feeling of an expensive pair of pants.

Kids will always fight the parents on wearing things they don't like. If you listen to their preferences, and for the most part only buy clothes that they want to wear, they'll have an easier time getting dressed and taking care of their things—and your life will be easier every single day. If they can learn to make responsible choices now, you won't have to do this with them forever. If you find something in the donate bin that you want them to keep—the sweater from their grandmother—ask them why it's in the donate pile. If the answer is reasonable—it's itchy—maybe Grammy can be guided toward brands your child likes, so waste is reduced.

Keep up with sorting through the clothing more frequently for smaller children (monthly for babies, every few months for toddlers, seasonally for bigger kids). This will make your life so much easier. It's half an hour of decision making versus trying to find an entire afternoon in your already packed schedule to go through everything.

Less is more in your kid's closet!

Creative Solutions

WENDY HAD A GREAT IDEA. She put a trundle bed in the room with the crib when it was a nursery. She planned for it to be her child's big-boy bed, but when he was a baby she used it for nursing him in the night and later to read stories to him. When it became his bed, she didn't put a mattress in the trundle part, but instead used it for storage. In the very beginning, she used it for all the baby shower gifts that weren't the right size yet, and later she used it for her child's toys. Her plan was to wait and put a mattress in it when he was old enough to have friends or cousins sleep over—but in the meantime (he was five when we met him), it was an awesome place for his toys, and he could easily toss everything in there.

Much like with toys, children's clothes also fall into the "less is more" category—though, also like toys, it's hard to stick with this. Just try to buy less, knowing that it means you'll have less to deal with on a daily basis. It might seem as if having more means you can do laundry less frequently and therefore will have less work to do . . . but that's not how it works. You end up with those monster loads of laundry where you end up folding forever. Fewer clothes and smaller loads of laundry done more frequently means you'll breeze through it.

Slightly older children, all the way up to teens, are able to be more self-sufficient and make choices more easily if there aren't a hundred items to choose from in their dressers and closets. They also are more likely to do their own laundry when they start running out of things to wear by the end of the week, instead of having enough to last for a month. A month-long pile of laundry will require your help; but they can handle a week's worth of dirty clothes.

Hand-me-downs

Here we are crushing your dreams again: The person to whom you're giving all the clothes your children have outgrown may not want your castoffs. Don't freak out! It's true!

We don't tell you this to bum you out and make you feel bad about all the stuff you've dumped on your cousin, neighbor, sister, sister-in-law, or friend. We tell you this because when we clear out our clients' children's bedrooms (and front hall closets) we often find clothes that make no sense for that particular child, which is why bags and bags of clothes don't even make it into the child's room. The sizes are wrong. The style is wrong. The season for the style and size are wrong. Nobody wants to be ungrateful or hurt anyone's feelings, so they keep accepting and you keep giving. Stop it.

When it comes to hand-me-downs, be as tough as you are when doing your own clothes. Don't give things that are torn, stained, or stretched out

Some clothes are worth saving and sharing, but not all!

of shape. Ask yourself, and the family that's going to be on the receiving end, what actually works for them. Maybe their girl doesn't like or wear dresses or party shoes—no matter how much you paid for them. Maybe your boy loves jeans and their boy won't wear them. Maybe the other family simply has enough hand-me-downs and doesn't want any more.

If you're keeping hand-me-downs for another child in your family, consider getting airtight bins. These are more expensive, but we've often thrown away piles of clothes that were perfectly good to begin with but were ruined by being stored in poor-quality bins that let in moisture or mice. If you're storing the bins of clothing inside your home (not in an attic, basement, or garage), then regular bins will likely do just fine.

Keep Your Children's Spaces Running Smoothly

For the most part, adults don't want to hang out in a playroom because it's boring for them and often uncomfortable. As a result, the playroom becomes an infrequently used room that is generally a dumping ground. After a thorough declutter, if the toys and games are put back in a way that children can easily help maintain, then it won't be such a dreaded place for adults.

We also believe that color coding of anything in a child's room/play space is unnecessary and often counterproductive. Kids have a hard enough time learning to put things away without disappointing you by messing up your systems. The time it takes to color-code children's toys, books, and clothes is more than we ever had as mothers. Coding by subject—blocks, cars, dolls, kitchen—is far more effective than color coding. We also love labeling bins and baskets with stickers or photos to help kids know where to put things away.

One of the most important parts of working in children's areas is creating systems specific to the age of the children. For this reason, the systems have to be designed to change over time and grow with the children. If the

PRO TIP:
Small Spaces

For many families, especially if they live in an apartment, the play area is in the living room and the kids have limited space in their bedrooms. There may also be a small area like a bookcase or two in the corner of the living room holding the child's things. In this situation, bins you *can't* see through are better than clear, especially if you have young children. They aren't putting their things away yet and you may not want to look at their brightly colored toys after they've gone to bed. Always label these bins well, not just with words but with pictures. Stickers or labels work well for things like cars, animals, and blocks. This helps the child to find toys and also put them away when they are a little older.

systems in the home are age appropriate (low-down hooks for backpacks, bins for shoes, and broad enough categories for toys) children will learn to put things away.

When there is a new baby in the house it is helpful to have everything you need for them right in the changing table; wipes and diapers, of course, but also keeping their clothes in a bin on the shelves of the changing table will help save time.

Out of frustration, parents often get to the point of simply doing giant purges when the children aren't around in hopes that they won't miss all the stuff being thrown away or donated. This works to eliminate some of the excess and is acceptable for toddlers—but it doesn't teach children ages four and up to think through what they actually want to keep and why. It also means that the teaching moments that can be used to prevent over-purchasing of plastic junk don't happen. This is why we suggest doing more frequent, smaller decluttering sessions with children rather than letting things get to this level of frustration and just tossing everything yourself.

Sentimental Items

"Save Forever" is what we label memorabilia bins. We take matters of the heart, especially when it comes to mothers, seriously. Over time you will cull what's in the bin—but don't overthink it when you put sentimental saves in there. As a new mother, you might over-save because the whole experience is new, and you think you'll want to remember it all. Later, as your baby becomes an actual person, you'll focus on saving things that remind you of who they were at a particular stage. Once a year go through the bins and toss the things that don't pull at your heart in any way or that don't interest you anymore. It's OK to get rid of those things. The goal is that someday, in the distant future, you'll have one (maybe large) bin that is an emotional record of who your child was to you. The goal is not to be able to stock the childhood wing of the presidential museum of your child should he or she become the president—leave that to the historians.

Myth Busted

"Having a playroom will make my life better."

IF YOU HAVE AN ACTUAL PLAYROOM, the law of unintended consequences comes into play. When playrooms are designated and designed, it's with the idea of children having a nice place to play and to do things that don't interest adults much. Unfortunately, in many cases children don't want to play there alone or even with other children. The trick is to make the playroom welcoming for adults as well. This can be as simple as putting a comfortable chair or a table and chairs for the adults so you can do other things while you're in the playroom.

Owning Well

Aim for well-made items that can grow with your child.

Kids' Storage

A strong, well-built storage unit, like an IKEA Kallax, is a wonderful Intentional Investment for a child's room or playroom. The ability to get toys and books off the floor is an efficient way to keep things organized. We recommend something that holds bins; you can purchase cute animal-themed bins for your little ones and switch them out for more sophisticated-looking bins as they get older.

Our best advice for Mindful Maintenance in a child's room is constant surveillance. It's good to keep this in mind when buying cheap things that are never going to last through more than one child. Yes, good toys are more expensive, but if they can be passed from child to child, the cost per use, and cost to the environment, is more reasonable. Also, be constantly aware of the toys your child no longer uses because the sooner you can donate them, the more likely another child will get the opportunity to enjoy them.

Eco Tips

High-quality toys, such as classic wooden cars and animals for toddlers, are a gift to yourself and your child. They last and last and they encourage play and creativity. And while we talked about hand-me-downs and donations not being appropriate all the time, something like a classic hand-carved toy (check out Etsy!) can be enjoyed for years by several different children.

Keep It Up!

Keeping the children's rooms tidy changes based on the age of the children who live there and the parent's tolerance for mess. Some children are naturally tidy, but the ones who don't care about putting their things away are more common. With young children, quick tidy-ups seem easier to us because of their short attention span. Leaving their rooms until hours are needed to put everything right will be difficult. As children grow they have a need for doing things their own way; and so teenage rooms look very different from their early childhood rooms. This is a good thing, but their rooms don't always look good. At that point you have to decide if you want to make your teenager clean up his or her room or you want to save your energy for something else. It takes almost zero energy to close the bedroom door and keep moving.

Home Office

A functional space for making sure your work
and your to-dos are getting done

YOUR HOME OFFICE SHOULD SET YOU UP FOR SUCCESS. Whether you have a full home office, one set up in your kitchen, or even a small desk in your bedroom—the goal is the same: to make the most of the time that you have to work. In addition to all the "work" work that gets accomplished in home offices, so many other items end up here. Everything from taxes and health care to school forms and thank-you notes is handled in this space.

There are real-life consequences to not paying taxes, not getting your children's camp forms in on time, and not submitting your health-care claims. Whereas a disorganized closet only makes getting dressed harder, a disorganized office flows into your life in the outside world. An office that is well organized and easy to use helps make all the chores handled there much less tedious.

Because of the wide range of purposes served, each home office is different. You could be a parent with a command center, a person with a full-time job who works from home, or someone running your own business from your home. Despite the many varied uses, the systems for making them high-functioning are the same. And when your systems are in place:

- **TIME IS SAVED WHEN YOU KNOW** exactly where the scissors, tape, and stamps are kept.
- **MONEY IS SAVED** when you don't pay late fees on bills that went missing.
- **FRIENDS AND FAMILY KNOW YOU CARE ABOUT THEM** when you respond to invitations in a timely manner.
- **THE STRESS AROUND TAX TIME IS GREATLY REDUCED** when you have organized, easy-to-find files.

How Do You Use Your Office?

When thinking through how to set up your home office, as with any other area, be realistic about who you are and how you will use the space:

- **DO YOU HAVE A JOB OUTSIDE THE HOME** or is this your full-time workspace?
- **DO YOU SHARE THE OFFICE WITH ANYONE?**
- **ARE YOU A PARENT** who needs a central base of operations?
- **ARE YOU PRIMARILY A PAPER PERSON** or a digital person?
- **DO YOU HOLD ON TO PAPERS LONGER THAN NECESSARY?** Are you sure?
- **IS YOUR OFFICE THE FAMILY DUMPING GROUND** for things no one knows what to do with?

Answering these questions will help you sort through the excess and help you organize in a way that works specifically for you and your household.

Where do you work? Does anything else happen in that space?

SORT AND DECIDE

If you run a business out of your home office we suggest doing personal papers and business papers separately. With both sections, the first project when tackling an office area is to gather all the paper together and categorize by subject (e.g., financial, catalogues, child-related) and then subcategorize (for example within the broad financial category you will have credit card statements, electricity bills, and mortgage-related papers). If you know you can find all of this information online with your bank or electric company log-in, plan to shred the paper. We recommend labeling a few boxes "SHRED"—smaller ones, as they'll be very heavy when full—and then you can easily toss paper in there. If there are important tax-related papers you cannot easily find online, we recommend keeping them for seven years. As always, and especially for any business-related papers, ask your accountant what should be kept as hard copies.

If you don't have a designated home office, carry all the paper to one room where you will be able to work over a number of sessions—and possibly over a number of days. The dining room can be a great place to put all the boxes and bags of paper (if you still have one after the renovation we discussed in the kitchen section!).

This is a great time to accept your partner's offer to help. If you've been shooing them away, saying you want to do this decluttering/purging thing yourself, remember: Paper is heavy! Ask for help if you need it.

Paper is the hardest, slowest part of household organization. Most pieces of paper have to at least be glanced at, if not read entirely; and there's a lot of them. The good news is that people have far less of it than they had even ten years ago when we started Done & Done Home. Even people who still read print newspapers and magazines don't clip and save articles as much as they once did. People are more comfortable with the idea that they'll be able to find what they need on the internet.

In the past, we helped people sort through files full of decades' worth of articles covering places they wanted to visit, recipes, advice for friends, and advice for themselves. The filing systems were quite impressive. Sometimes file cabinets filled whole rooms. Retired doctors and lawyers held on to files that they or a client or patient might need. Writers held on to paper of all sorts to help them trace their way back in time or move them forward through an idea to a completed article or manuscript. Over time, files

Some papers just need to be saved!

were removed from the actual file drawers and placed in file boxes, which then filled closets, attics, basements, and shelves in storage rooms and garages. That behavior is coming to an end, as people learn to scan their files and also to rely on the internet—but many still need to confront that transition, or help their parents do so. Scanning most of your old personal papers/old bills is really not worthwhile; just have courage and shred them.

SCARY BAGS

If you're already nodding your head when you read the words "scary" and "bag" together, you don't need this explanation—but for everybody else, a scary bag is a tote or shopping bag full of paper to-dos or have-dones or will-dos of all sorts. Magazines with the corner of the pages turned down for that possible trip, invitations, bills, receipts for returns, receipts to remember where that shop is, tickets, playbills, perhaps letters and cards—and always business cards. The scariest thing about scary bags is that where there is one, there will be more. It's a way of life. To handle them: Dump them all out and get sorting in the usual way—like-with-like and then subcategorize. Much of what is in the bag will now be so far in the past that it will be easier to let go of the paper.

PAPER HOLDER-ON-ERS

Paper storage can look great.

People who hold on to paper tend to be some of our brightest clients. Their smarts often result in an industrious approach to information. An idea crosses their mind while reading and they think of somebody who could benefit from the knowledge. They fold the corner of the magazine or put a star next to the article. They're reading the physical newspaper because

they still get it delivered. They suspect they're missing things in the digital copy and they're just that thorough.

Those who hold on to paper often have a fear of forgetting something that could potentially be useful. If you live with a person who has a problem with paper, try and see all the good in what they do.

DECLUTTERING PAPER

Bills, Saved Documents, and Magazines

Back to those stacks of files, boxes, and scary bags that are now stacked in your dining room or around your kitchen table. If you or a person you live with holds on to a lot of paper, it is crucial that you block out enough time to go through each piece.

Old filing cabinets will inevitably be time consuming, so pace yourself and don't get boggged down examining every paper and file. There can be some categorization and subcategorization to move things along but a subcategory like credit card statements is far harder to deal with than electric bills. Start with the easier categories and save the hardest for the end when you have built up your to-be-shred muscle.

Even if you accept the idea that the electric bill can be viewed online, you still may not be ready to switch to paperless billing—but you might be willing to set up a new hybrid system where you receive a paper bill in the mail, pay the bill online, and then shred it rather than file it.

If you are willing to get rid of years of electric bills, you might want to shred anything with your information on it, at least in the beginning. Identity theft is a concern that some paper people have, so baby steps at first. Not all of this is rational. If we explain to you that the magazine with your address label has already been seen by many people in order to get the magazine delivered to your home, and that therefore taking off every label and shredding it is not necessary, our rationale won't help if you have a gripping fear of identity theft.

Create simple, logical categories.

Hide the
clutter
elegantly.

What usually happens when someone has these sorts of fears is that not only do the labels stay; the magazines and newspapers stay also. Sorting too quickly can backfire when dealing with Paper Holder-on-ers, so for round one remove the address labels, recycle the magazines and newspapers, and shred the address labels. Then set up a new system where the mail comes into the house: Promise yourself that you won't read the paper or the magazines until you remove the labels. Maybe put a small basket or bin by the mail table so you remember to remove them right away. Keep a shredder in your office or under the mail table in your front hall and shred envelopes with your personal information.

Go slowly with paper to avoid the sinking feeling that you threw something away that you might need later, something that you didn't look at carefully. This feeling can result in a more general paralysis about throwing paper in the trash or shredding it. The goal is to work on the feelings as much as the stacks, bags, and boxes of paper—so take your time.

If you don't have any issues around paper but it simply got out of control, put it in categories such as magazines, business or personal files, and mail that needs to be handled, and then divide into subcategories (e.g., bills that haven't been paid, invites that haven't been answered), and put the magazines into like-with-like piles.

You may care less about that celebrity marriage when the *People* magazine stack is up to your knee. Although you may think you're going to read those thirty issues of the *New Yorker*, you'd have to quit your job and go to a cabin in the woods to get it done—so consider recycling those too (and remember the archives are online).

Shredding

There are ways to handle nerves about sensitive information that don't involve fires in the backyard and garbage disposals. If you have a few bags of paper to be shredded when you're done with the paper project, you can take the bags to an office supply store like Staples and put the paper in locked bins to be shredded later. If that makes you nervous or if you have so much paper that taking it somewhere seems impossible, you can call a shredding company and they will come and pick it up at your house. They use locked bins to collect it and if you want to watch them shred it for your own peace of mind, find a company that shreds on the truck. If the whole idea of your personal information (bank statements, credit card statements, address labels) leaving your home makes you a nervous wreck, find a shredding company that works with banks, law firms, and credit card companies. If you think *you're* nervous, just imagine how much *they* don't want that information out in the general public.

Pens and Pencils

Why does something so small and so useful get its own paragraph? They're not causing much trouble in the pen holder, the junk drawer, the desk, or in your handbag, right? Wrong. They're everywhere and they keep coming. Throwing half of the pens you own into the garbage right now would make your home feel lighter and more organized. Is there a sort of

Weed out the pens and pencils that work, and keep them together.

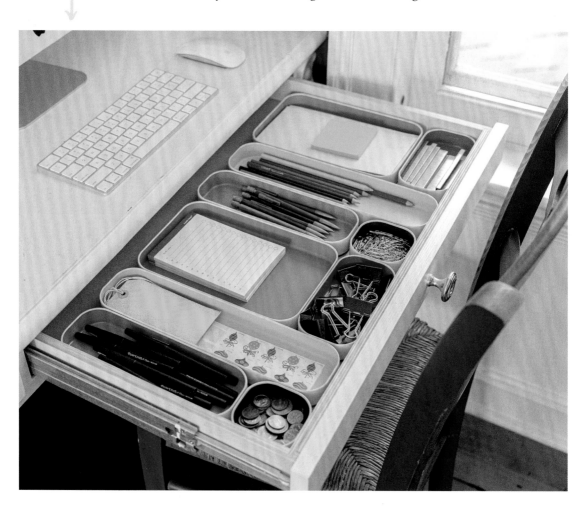

When Clutter Is Cool

IN ALMOST ALL CASES, we'd say that productivity increases with a high-functioning office—but we organized the office of John, an incredibly productive artist who is considered to be an American treasure. His workspace was full of all sorts of things and there wasn't complete order anywhere; but far be it from us to criticize his systems—clearly, they worked for him. Organizing isn't one-size-fits-all and, as long as the space isn't hurting anyone else, we think it's OK for things to be a bit nutty!

The way to measure the sanity of this choice is the output of the person living that way. Wrote the Great American Novel? Keep on doing you. Paying huge fines for late taxes, unpaid parking tickets, and credit card fees? Time to clean it up and create new systems.

When you have a desk with drawers it helps prevent clutter on the surface!

pen you always choose when you can find it? Treat yourself to a box of those and get rid of the ones from the gas station and the bank that barely work.

Photographs

Physical photos are a big problem for anybody who ever had a camera that wasn't on their phone. Most people are unclear about how to sort and save them. The whole problem seems unwieldy because it takes up so much space.

Many of our clients have bags and boxes of loose photos and many, many photo albums. Depending on the age of the client, those may include not just their personal albums, but also albums they've inherited from parents or grandparents.

We suggest the Photo Project be treated as completely separate from the Great Purge you're working on now. We also suggest that you bring some basic order to the project but save it for what we think of as a "cold winter's eve." If you live in a warm place this could be something you do when it's so hot outside that you'd rather be inside.

Creating order includes leaving the albums you enjoy on shelves where you can find them. All other albums and loose photos should be stored in airtight bins so that if the project isn't completed for a long period of time, you don't risk the photos getting ruined. Don't store them in bins that are very deep. Photos are heavy.

Put the bins in a place that matches your time expectation and, as always, try to separate fantasy from reality. For example, if you think you're going to get to this in the next few months, you can leave this entire project in the bottom of a closet close to where you will do the sorting. The truth is, it takes a long time to go through photos because they're memory prompters. That's why people hold on to them and why it's hard to get rid of them.

Once you're ready to get started, categorize photos into piles by periods of time and subcategorize by event and by family. This means that all your wedding photos that didn't make it into the album are one pile and your son's graduation photos are another. Grouping them like this will make it easier to choose the best ones and ditch the rest. It also helps with the worry of forgetting someone, somewhere, something. Give yourself a lot of time for this part of the project.

Sort through the first bin, but don't consider it completely finished. Do every bin once and then, when the photos are fresh in your mind, like a giant game of Concentration, try to match stacks of loose photos with the events in the albums. The best photos are likely to be in there.

Depending on how your albums were put together (corners versus sticky pages), you may want to take the albums apart and have the photos digitally scanned to reduce the space they take up in your home. You can also make albums that are streamlined (like Apple Photo books) and that take up less space on the shelves. If you have children, it's also a very easy way to make them each an album of important family photos since you can get multiple copies of the album.

You will likely end up with lots of photos that aren't scanned and aren't in albums. These may be Save Forever—and that's fine. We've often helped families where entire photo albums are thrown away because nobody has any idea who the people in the photos are. We suggest that you write on the back in pencil who the people are. Use full names—not just Pete but Peter Smith—and if it's an older photo, perhaps a middle name as well. If someone in your family is later interested in genealogy, this will make their research easier.

As you make your way through these steps, your piles will get smaller. You'll combine bins so the entire project will be reduced. Eventually you will probably end up with a bin or two and will feel you can go no further. As long as all the photos in the bin are clearly labeled, there's nothing wrong with saving some loose photos!

Technology

It's hard to imagine that technology is its own category—but it is. The world can be divided into two groups—those who believe any cable can be replaced, and those who make it a personal challenge to keep every single one and are deeply satisfied when they match one to its device every so often.

Let's say you are in the first group and your spouse is in the second group. You're probably going to be living with some big bins of cords and old remotes, not to mention your spouse's original iPhone and its box. The tech itself is a battle you can't win—but there are a few things you can do to make the clutter more manageable.

Start with boxes: Do the research so you can show that keeping the Apple boxes might increase the value slightly should you decide to sell them; but is

Drawers are also useful for tech accessories and cords.

it enough that you need to store all those boxes for years? An iPhone box is small and might seem like it's not a big deal, but the desktop PC box? That's another story. There is no reason to keep these boxes unless you are moving soon or plan to sell your computer and that's only because they are designed to protect the computers during shipping, not because they add value.

Apple boxes are truly a tech clutter subcategory. They are a design marvel. So clean! So high-functioning, with our expensive tech product

nestled into its little home when it arrives! But does that mean we have to keep every single box? If you or your significant other decides you do want to keep all the boxes, consider putting them in airtight bins.

The real trick to tech management is learning how to dispose of tech items properly, by finding out who recycles what and then doing it regularly, so you aren't faced with a computer graveyard and trying to wipe clean a bunch of old computers somewhere down the road.

The next big category is cords. We want to say just recycle them all (cords are considered electrical waste) but we know that will never happen. Most of our clients admit they have seldom, or never, gotten a cord out of the bin though they've dragged the bin around for years, from house to house. It's going to take you at least an hour, so maybe set this job up with Netflix running. Separate them like-with-like so you don't keep duplicates. Take a good, hard look at each cord. Get rid of the power cords from old laptops. All the Apple cords from old iPods and Shuffles can go. All the phone-charging cords for the phones that are long gone. Ideally, you will end up with a small bin full of wound-up charging cords for current devices.

We know technology and the clutter that comes with it is likely here to stay, but it doesn't have to stay in your living room or, even worse, your bedroom. If there is no reasonable place to store it because you live in an apartment or an older home with limited closet space, try asking yourselves what each item is actually adding to your life and what you're giving up to keep it.

Go out of your way to avoid lost or tangled computer cords!

CREATE A KITCHEN COMMAND CENTER

Many of our clients are moms with children at home who chose to have an area in the kitchen to organize everyday life. There is no sense in having your mom-office in another space since there is so much time spent in the kitchen between meal prep and eating and overseeing homework.

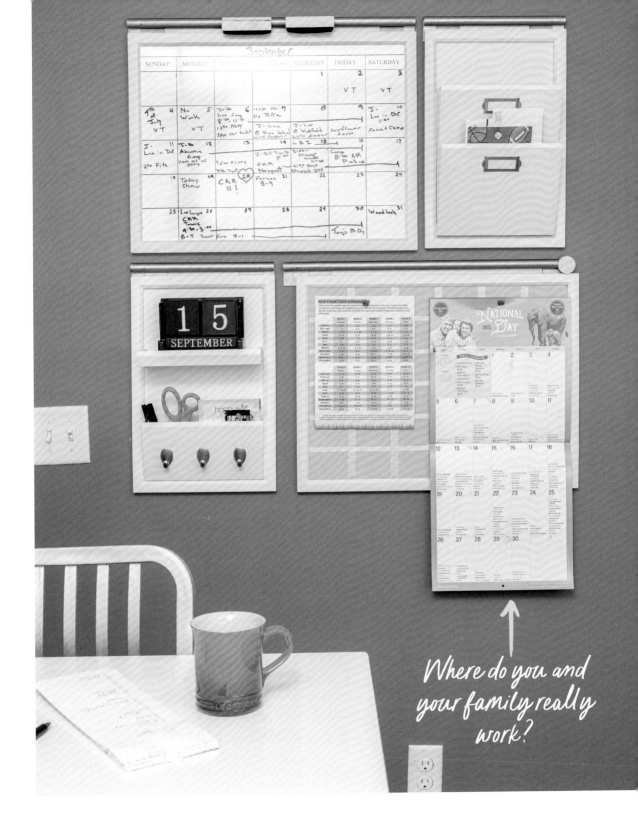

Where do you and your family really work?

Creating a Closet Command Center

THERE DOESN'T NEED TO BE A GIANT OFFICE dedicated to just work in any home—sometimes a little creative thinking goes a long way. Beth had four children going in different directions at all times and only had a tiny ten-inch shelf for her mom command center. She ripped out a closet in the family room off the kitchen that had housed toys and games from when they were little and turned it into a closet-office.

The command center can be either a small desk or, like in Kate's house, the bottom shelf of a kitchen cabinet. Because she doesn't need much space for her ten pieces of paper, it's still the area where both she and her husband can put any sort of to-dos for family life like bills, camp forms, and invitations. It's also where she keeps notes about James for the babysitter. (She also keeps a small bin of extra phone charger cords in there, because it's one of those things that she doesn't want to spend ten minutes looking for—but she knows she's going to need eventually.) If everything is organized properly, children can be taught that if they have something that needs the attention of a parent, this is where it should go.

Make it easy to find the things you use most.

The family calendar can be hung up here or, if everybody is old enough, you can share an online calendar for the whole family. Either way, the shared family calendar makes busy family life so much easier to handle. You can keep track of all your appointments and commitments, plus anything for the children. Maybe someday you'll spy a wide-open day in the calendar and book the appointment to use the gift card for the massage that you've been carrying around in your wallet for a year . . . or two.

If you're lucky enough to have an actual desk in the kitchen, there will be space for envelopes, petty cash, pens and pencils, paper clips, and maybe even a small printer for last-minute forms so you don't have to go to another room to print.

Take a minute to think of all the last-minute, aggravating things that happen in your home in the morning when you're trying to get out the door. There will be some things that are specific to your family. This is the place to prepare for the inevitably stressful exit.

Myth Busted

"I have to keep all papers related to my taxes for seven years."

IT'S TRUE—BUT YOU CAN KEEP THESE DIGITALLY. If you were to need any old statements, you would be able to go online and print them out. You can scan much of what you need to save and put it in one folder labeled Taxes and the relevant year. It's best to keep one box of all tax-related information but now that so much of financial life is digital, one box can contain a large envelope for each year of items that weren't easy to scan. At the end of each tax year, gather everything together and get it out of your bill-paying/paper-dealing area. Boxes like these can be kept in an attic or basement or in the back of a closet since you won't need them frequently (if ever).

Keep Your Office Running Smoothly

For years now, we've seen that the design trend with desks is to be sleek, with no drawers or maybe one very thin one. You may be able to keep some stamps and a pen in there. The truth is that you need storage to hold everything from pens and paper to cards and envelopes, plus checkbooks, electronics, and more. The sleek drawer-less desk becomes a mountain of visible clutter, and these distractions make it hard to accomplish anything. If your desk didn't come with drawers, consider adding a freestanding set of drawers underneath it.

It can be helpful to set up a physical in-box or drop-off station that works for your family for paperwork, bills, or anything that needs your response.

If you learn what documents you actually need to save as physical paper versus scanning or even shredding, it will keep saved paper to a minimum, which will help things run smoothly.

Scanning is an excellent choice if you are someone who can keep things digitally organized. It does not help if your computer is a black hole.

Once you've eliminated all the things you don't need to keep, you will be left with a much more manageable work area.

If you are someone who likes to hold on to paper, make sure you can find what you're looking for.

Owning Well

A quality desk chair is worth the investment!

Desk Chair

With more and more people working from home and spending a good deal of time in their home office, some Intentional Investments may be in order. The number-one thing we suggest is a good, comfortable desk chair.

Whether that's an ergonomic chair that allows you to work in comfort or a standing desk, it's worth paying a little more. Research shows that the more you care for your physical body during your workday, the more productive you can be. Now is not the time to grab that old rickety, leftover dining-room chair that you inherited from dear Aunt Sally; you'll pay for that decision in the long run.

Eco Tips

The good news is many of the items we use in our home offices are recyclable! You do need to know, however, that most of them cannot be put in your curbside recycling:

- **PRINTER CARTRIDGES** can be taken to your local office supply store, such as Staples or Best Buy. Not every store accepts every type of cartridge, so call ahead or check online to save yourself any aggravation.
- **CORDS, CABLES, WIRES, AND RECHARGE-ABLE BATTERIES** can be recycled at Best Buy. They typically have a kiosk at the front of the store where you can drop off that tangled mess. Again, call ahead or check on their website to make sure they'll take your castoffs.
- **FOR BIGGER ITEMS, LIKE COMPUTERS AND PRINTERS,** you'll likely have to take a trip to your local recycling center. It's an extra step, but just dumping them in the trash will leave you feeling guilty and may actually prevent you from getting rid of those items at all. Better a morning spent

dealing with those things properly than years of them sitting in the basement or garage.

Keep It Up!

Once your paperwork is organized, a good time to do a yearly sweep is just after tax time. Because you're gathering all necessary paperwork together and either doing your taxes or sending it off to the accountant, you will know what you need to keep and what you can shred or recycle. If you make the time each year to quickly dispose of what you don't need and straighten up what you're keeping, your office space will be high functioning all year.

Storage
Spaces

Basements, attics, and garages that support your life

STORAGE SPACES WORK LIKE A DINGHY FOR A SHIP: While probably not important every day, if they're not functioning properly, there will be problems later.

These areas are crucial to a high-functioning home. One of the reasons living in an apartment is so much more organizationally challenging is that you tend not to have these bigger spaces. But wherever you live, once these spaces are orderly and working in sync, everyday life in the home can function smoothly.

People tend to treat all of their storage spaces as interchangeable rather than as designated areas. For example, the garage should hold backup household items and tools, while the basement could house holiday items and hand-me-downs, and the attic is for long-term storage and Save Forever. Confusion, over-purchasing, and frustration happen when these various systems are not sorted and nothing is with its group. Sometimes people hold on to too much because these spaces allow for that—but that can be fixed.

In choosing a storage space, make sure to consider climate: If your attic is not insulated, or your basement floods, then these are not good spaces for storing many items.

If you live in an apartment building, you might have storage in the basement. If you live in a condo or townhome, you may pay for storage offsite. Since these storage spaces often cost extra money and tend to be a lot smaller than garages or attics, it's even more important to follow the guidelines here. We completely understand the need for extra storage when your home doesn't have space for things like holiday decorations or family memorabilia, but there is no need to pay for an inch more than you really need.

Your garage doesn't have to be saved for your car.

Organized storage matters because:

- **YOU'LL SAVE MONEY ON HOLIDAY DECORATIONS** because you know what you have.
- **YOU'LL SAVE TIME** finding what you need.
- **YOU'LL SAVE MONEY ON SPORTING GOODS** because you can see what's there.
- **YOU'LL BE ABLE TO PARK YOUR CAR** in the garage.
- **YOU'LL MAKE SURE** that Save Forever items are stored properly so they don't get ruined.

Approximately one-third of Americans can't fit a car in their garage. And it's not the size of the garage preventing the cars from fitting; there's simply too much in there. If these areas aren't packed full, you can enjoy them for other things! One of our clients turned her garage into a gym and another transformed a basement storage room into an awesome playroom.

Are you using these items enough to keep them around?

How Do You Use
Your Storage Spaces?

Some storage items are things you only use seasonally, like holiday decorations or beach and pool items—and that's a perfect use of extra space. Nobody wants their synthetic Christmas tree, Halloween decorations, or rafts and floats piled up in their living spaces or closets.

And then there are items someone once used—soccer gear, tennis rackets, golf clubs, bicycles—that are perfectly good and could be used again, so they stay. Unless, of course, the person who used the soccer gear was twelve at the time, is now nineteen or thirty, and will likely never play soccer again. As with every other part of the house, the faster you donate items from the garage, the likelier there will be someone else who can use it.

Items in storage are almost always *decisions deferred*. Do any of these scenarios sound familiar?

- **YOU AND YOUR PARTNER CAN'T REACH AN AGREEMENT** about whether or not an item should go. Because items that go are gone forever, they're often allowed to stay, but not in the living area of the home—so they go to a storage area.
- **A CHILD IS UNABLE TO LET GO OF A TOY** but doesn't use it anymore, so you just skip the battle and put the item in the basement, garage, or attic. That may make sense for a period of time, but when the children who owned the toys are grown and living in their own homes, consider reducing this collection. We know you won't get rid of all of it because you're saving it for your future grandchildren, but do try to condense it to a bin or two.

SORT AND DECIDE

Since these spaces tend to be intertwined, we suggest organizing them all at the same time, sorting into categories like sentimental items, holiday items, tools, sports equipment, and toys. By bringing everything together from these different areas and putting them with their group, you can start to get a sense of how much you really have.

As with all decluttering, pull every single thing out and sort like-with-like. That means: all sporting items together and then subcategories according to the actual sport. Toys can be subcategorized by age or by child. Keep a section for items that you know will absolutely stay, like new camping equipment or current sports equipment—but don't put those back in the garage yet. It's a big space but it can easily be overrun if storage needs aren't well thought out and implemented before you start putting things back.

Review all the outdoor toys and get rid of the ones that are no longer useful to your children.

Think about how and when you use things, and put them back accordingly.

When was the last time you went to the beach or the pool?

Go through any bins of hand-me-downs and, if you missed the boat on any items but they're still in decent shape, donate them.

Holiday Decorations

Holiday decor is one of the hardest things to declutter. The items are often infused with wonderful memories and each and every piece can appear to be sentimental. The truth is, some things may feel special but you have to ask yourself if that's actually true. If you're running out of space for all of your decorations, you're going to have to make some decisions. Our advice is to choose a category, say Christmas ornaments, and put every single one you own together where you can see them all. Choose your top five absolute must keeps—the first ornament you and your partner bought

together, the snowman your son made in kindergarten, the star topper from your childhood tree, etc. Set those five aside and take a look at what's left. Now choose the five that you know you won't miss. The random filler balls that you picked up at Walmart, the plastic icicles you thought would look nice but you never actually liked, and the weird-looking elf you got in a company secret Santa swap. Put those in a donation box and start the whole process over again.

We're not going to lie, it's going to be a hard process. One way to make it easier going forward is to be incredibly intentional about what you purchase in the future. Never buy something simply because it's on sale, and commit to the "one in, one out" rule. If you see something in the store and you think you must have it, know that when you get home, you'll have to get rid of a similar item you already own. You may surprise yourself by how much you actually don't love that little tchotchke in the store!

The Big Three (or Four) Storage Areas

Most homes have at least one garage, attic, or basement (and sometimes storage rooms in the home or offsite storage); some have all four. What's important to keep in mind is that they're used in very similar ways, with a couple of differences.

The things that are put in these rooms or places tend to be stuff we want to keep though we may not use it, or may not use it frequently, and that's great. That's how storage is designed to be used.

In an ideal world, cars would fit in garages, attics would all be climate controlled and easily accessed by a real staircase, basements would never

Make your attic a place where things are saved, not forgotten.

SAVE FOREVER
JACK

SAVE FOREVER
HUDSON

SAVE FOREVER
PETER

SAVE FOREVER
LILY

GIRL - WINTER
SIZE 18-24 MONTHS

GIRL - SUMMER
SIZE 12-12 MONTHS

MATERNITY

flood, and storage rooms would never get mice or bugs in them. Sadly, we don't live in that organizational paradise. Here in the real world, we keep our cars outdoors all winter long and climb rickety attic ladders that we pull down by a dangling string. We throw out boxes of yearbooks and holiday decorations because they got soaked through and we set mice catch-and-release traps because we don't see ourselves as murderous monsters (even though we're certain that when we release them to the wild they meet with their friends and make a plan to come back to our house because we didn't kill them the first time).

Sentimental Items: Inherited Belongings

Let's dig in with one of the biggest problems we see in storage areas of all sorts—inherited belongings—and we will bounce around a little among the four different storage areas.

These items were given to someone by someone else, often an older family member. The first someone didn't say "No, thank you" because, at the heart of the giving, there was kindness and often a memory. So, Aunt Nancy's china or Grandpa's chair, which both sort of fit and are harmless enough, stay in the attic, basement, garage, or storage room.

The big challenges arise when a close relative dies and there is no time to go through the items in that person's home. Fair enough. Nobody wants to keep paying rent on an apartment where nobody is living or get stuck with the house for another year of property taxes and mortgage payments.

What often happens is, just short of packing actual garbage, everything is boxed up and put in one of their children's basement, garage, or attic. Nobody wants to handle all those decisions in a time of grief. And, once the grief lets up, almost nobody wants to sit with their now deceased relative's stuff and try to decide what to keep and what to donate or trash, not to mention the overwhelming worry that somebody else in the family may want something.

I assure you we're not talking about Picassos, wads of cash, stacks of signed first editions, and big diamond rings. Your sister is already wearing the ring and the signed first edition is on your shelf. Your brother took the Picasso because he's a banker and he could afford the estate tax. What's left is the Pyrex, Mom's furs that nobody wants, your comic books that she held on to for you, records that are mostly scratched, lots of books, linens, and perhaps some china and silver that you intend to sell.

Not every saved item is a treasure.

Your dad might've been a big golfer, but are you?

The thing is, feelings are real even if the Pyrex is chipped and the records are warped. You remember that there was a time when Dad put a record on the turntable while Mom got the good china out and set the table for a dinner party. While you and your siblings listened to the laughter from your place on the stairs, the magical world of adult life unfolded in the dining room below you. There was a time when life wasn't so busy. Are you really supposed to drop the reminders of this time off at Goodwill? How are you supposed to know if your daughter will want them when she's grown?

So, decisions remain deferred while you scrape the ice and snow off the car for another winter because the car can't fit in the garage. You even consider moving because, though you love your house and your neighborhood, if you had more space—a bigger basement, or a walk-in attic, or even another garage—maybe you could keep everything in there and still park your car.

And that's when you realize why self-storage is a nearly $40 billion industry in the United States.

We'd love to help you keep that money in your bank account. If you're thirty-five years old now and paying over $100 a month for storage, you could easily spend $60,000 or more if you live to be eighty-five without dealing with your storage problem. We know for sure your heirs would rather have that money than whatever it is you've been storing at the self-storage place on Route 3.

Our suggestion is that you don't think of this as a "getting rid of" exercise but rather as a "reducing the amount you hold on to and whatever you keep, make it count" exercise. The underlying fear is of forgetting your loved one or in some less clear way, not valuing what they valued. People often think they should do this one box at a time because that seems to make sense, but the truth is, until you can really see everything you kept, you don't know what you have and your desire to hold on to more will be greater.

Let's say you have a wall of boxes in the garage that came from your mother's house. Perhaps you can discuss it with your spouse in a calm moment and say that you know the boxes are driving them crazy and you're going to attempt to handle it, but you need some help. The help you need involves being left alone and covered for the time it will take, which could be all afternoon. Don't rush this.

Have a couple of airtight bins ready so you can pack up the things you're going to keep as Save Forever items. Have some newspaper, bubble wrap, or tissue if you think you'll need it. Some people like to rewrap the items they're keeping in the original newspaper because it was Mom's local paper, and it also has the date on it from when she originally wrapped it up.

Also have a box of contractor bags for garbage. You can also use the old boxes to get rid of the things you aren't keeping.

If you have an extraordinarily patient friend, spouse, or maybe even one of your children, it's nice to have somebody to tell the stories to while you make the decisions. If you can't think of anybody who could sit with you for as long as it takes, then do it alone. You've got your memories to keep you company.

Make a lot of space in the garage or attic and begin unpacking everything in like-with-like piles. Once it is all unpacked and in piles, take a look and ask yourself, If I could only keep one thing, and that thing had to be in my home where I could see it or use it, what would that be? Take your time. Shop carefully. Once you've chosen your one thing, think about where in your house it's going to go.

It's nice to have something that you use all the time, like a letter opener from your dad's desk. You don't need to be overwhelmed with memory every time you sort the mail, but it's nice to use it and think of your dad. If you're worried that a relative might want something, and it's getting in the way of making decisions, and if it isn't crazy complicated emotionally to do so, ask them the same question. If they could have one thing that belonged to your mother, what would it be? You'd be surprised how often people want something that doesn't have monetary value. It may be something like that small blue bowl she kept on her desk for paper clips. If it's your dad's things, it may be his hammer or a money clip. It's often simple objects that someone touched and used every day.

Now that you've chosen the most precious objects for yourself and perhaps others, put into bags or boxes all the things that you don't want but

We always prefer clear bins and use the airtight ones if the storage space is not climate controlled. This can be true for attics, basements, and garages—and also for offsite storage. These containers require bold labeling with accurate details about what is inside so that time is not wasted looking for specific things. Keep categories together, like holiday bins, hand-me-downs, children's toys, and Save Forever items. You'll have a much easier time finding things quickly in the future.

Bring that crystal out of the attic and down to where you can enjoy it!

Old toys can find new life in your kid's room.

that could still be useful to somebody else. As you do so, put into garbage bags anything that is stained, broken, or too dirty to clean. Take the time to load the donation items into your car and take a couple of bags of garbage to the garbage area.

Once you've completed those steps, start them again. Of the things that are left to be sorted, choose one more thing. It's really two things now because you kept one thing on the first round of choosing; but let your emotions guide you in the exact same way. Choose as if it's the one precious thing you're going to keep to remind you of your person. Think again about where this special thing is going to go in your house.

If there's no room to display the item or use it in your home, and you're thinking of wrapping the item up and putting it into your Save Forever airtight bin, know that you're keeping this item just to keep it. That may be OK. Sometimes just having something in our lives and knowing exactly where it is, though we are never going to use it, is a comfort. Wrap it and set it in the bin and then take another pass at all the remaining items.

Take a moment here to congratulate yourself on how much you've accomplished. Though it only takes a few minutes to read this and think about how to declutter inherited belongings, the time it takes to actually accomplish the steps above could be hours or days. Don't worry about that. What's a couple of hours compared to the years those boxes have been in your garage, attic, or basement?

Do the steps as many times as you need to—choosing one special item as if it's the only one you're keeping and think about where it's going to go—and when you get to a place of truly feeling you don't want to let go of one more thing, start packing things into a Save Forever bin. Instead of just writing "Mom's things" on the label, write a quick list like "Mom's

Downsizing Decisions

BEFORE WE MET HER, MARY HAD DOWNSIZED from the large family apartment where she'd raised her family to her current one-bedroom place. She had hired a moving company to pack up all the beautiful furniture, dishes, books, art, and other items she thought her children might want someday. In deciding how much to spend on storage, she "saved" money by not paying for the climate-controlled room. We were hired to help her go through the storage and send pictures of things to her family to see what they would like. She hadn't been there in a while; and when we opened the storage room, it was clear right away that something was wrong. At some point a great deal of moisture had gotten into the storage locker, and over the years, it had destroyed many items. The upholstered furniture was beyond repair—and even many of the pieces of wooden furniture were warped. Some of the art had mold on it. These were not priceless treasures, but they had meaning to Mary and her family, and much of it was now garbage. We were heartbroken for her and, since then, we have made it our mission to keep this from happening to other people.

things: small silver items, blue teacups, eight books, two pairs of gloves, black handbag." Put the bins in a place where you don't come across them in your everyday life but you know exactly where they are. Attics and back rooms in the basement are great for these sorts of bins. Garages are OK, but if it means potentially scraping the snow and ice off your car for the rest of your life, find another spot. Spend the money on quality bins that seal properly and get them off the floor where possible. This is now your precious collection, and you don't want it to get ruined by heat, water, mice, or bugs.

All the Rest: Sports Equipment, Gardening Tools, Seasonal Items, and Outside Gear

So, now that the hard work is done, finding a day to handle the old bikes and toys (and the punctured pool float and the broken badminton net) sure seems easy.

Zones are the secret to a well-kept storage space.

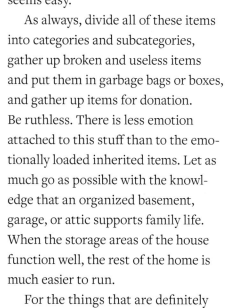

As always, divide all of these items into categories and subcategories, gather up broken and useless items and put them in garbage bags or boxes, and gather up items for donation. Be ruthless. There is less emotion attached to this stuff than to the emotionally loaded inherited items. Let as much go as possible with the knowledge that an organized basement, garage, or attic supports family life. When the storage areas of the house function well, the rest of the home is much easier to run.

For the things that are definitely staying, now is the time to go through all of those items.

Holiday decorations don't need to look perfect on the shelf—but you should make sure you actually want to keep all of them before storing them.

What do you
use when you
do what you do?

Tools

We recommend sorting tools where they are stored in your home. They're often small but heavy. If the person who owns most of the tools is interested, once everything else is out of the garage or basement, go back in and sort them on the floor, like-with-like. For people who don't often use tools, sorting with someone who does can be a maddening experience because they will always say—and they are right about this—that this tool or that screw is perfectly good. You can't argue with that.

People who own a lot of tools usually see themselves as people who are ready to handle problems. They're willing and able and they want to be ready, so throwing out or donating something they may need makes them unhappy. Their dad's hammer may also hold sentimental value. If there's one space where tidy, labeled bins aren't necessarily the answer, it's here. It may feel messy to you if you like perfect order, but it isn't wrong. A cluttered workbench is just another way of keeping things. If it drives you mad, try not to look at it.

Your go-to tool bag doesn't have to house every single tool you own.

Keep Your Storage Spaces Running Smoothly

Once you've sorted and purged, put the items that were in bins back where they belong and label them with detail as necessary. You may need to buy a few more bins at this point or perhaps you can reuse ones that have been emptied. Try to get rid of cardboard boxes if possible. Carboard doesn't hold up well with any moisture and critters love cardboard, so whatever you're keeping in them might eventually be ruined.

For all the things that are staying and belong in the garage, attic, or basement, you can now organize them properly. You can get shelving for the bins or install a wall system with hooks for everything. You can hang up ladders, scooters, pool noodles, and sports equipment of all sorts. Having a place off the floor for most things makes the storage spaces much easier to handle.

We also suggest keeping an inventory on your phone of what's in each space. You can do this easily by taking photos of the bin labels. This way you know where things are and where to put them back after using them.

Myth Busted

"If I had more storage space, everything would be better and I'd be happier."

IF YOU HAD MORE STORAGE SPACE, you'd simply have more stuff that you don't want in your living spaces. Storage is usually full of decisions deferred; the more storage space you have the fewer decisions you will force yourself to make. The real trick to having more space and being happier is to buy less and be ruthless about what you keep.

Owning Well

"Like with like" works for storing as well as sorting.

Storage Spaces

Clear airtight bins are best for all of these storage areas, but if you already have lots of colored plastic bins use those with detailed labels. Moving forward, if you find you need more bins, the higher-quality, weathertight bins will make a world of difference. The tight-fitting lids are weatherproof and critter-proof, and the lids won't collapse when you stack them.

If you have the space (or need the space!), some sturdy shelving is a great Intentional Investment. If you don't have high-quality bins, getting any boxes you have off the floor and onto those shelves is vitally important to protecting your possessions.

At the end of every season, it's a good idea to check over all of your seasonal tools and machines for any Mindful Maintenance needs. When summer ends, make sure your gardening tools are clean, your hoses are stored properly, and your lawn mower blades are free from grass and debris. Properly cover and store any outdoor furniture—yes, it's just snow—yes, it will absolutely shorten the life span of those chairs and tables. Bring in your umbrella and put it in a place where it won't get crushed or misshapen.

The same routine should be followed in the spring with all of your winter tools. Snow blowers, shovels, ice melt—all the things that won't be used for six months or so—should be carefully looked over before they're put away for the season.

Eco Tips

As you get your storage areas in order, particularly your garage, you'll be more likely to enjoy your yard. Our best eco tip is to use your newly organized spaces to create a yard that is environmentally friendly. Plant some flowers that will attract pollinators, add a bird feeder

or two, maybe even grow some vegetables! Once you can find your trowel and have easy access to your hose, puttering around in your yard can be a relaxing pastime rather than a stressful unwanted chore.

Keep It Up!

We recommend an annual sweep of each space. We do the garage in the fall, the attic in the spring, and basement in the winter.

You're probably thinking all we do is organize! Honestly, with each passing year we spend less and less time organizing because we are pretty well streamlined at this point and, because we stay on top of it, we can get through even these big areas quickly. This is what we wish for you! An organized home that is easy to manage so you have time to do the things you love.

Acknowledgments

KATE—I SIMPLY COULDN'T ASK FOR ANYTHING MORE FROM YOU. You are the hardest-working person I know and you do it all with good cheer. I can't believe my luck in having you for a daughter.

Mark—the sacrifice you made in leaving your country for mine is never far from my mind. Thank you for supporting me and Kate every single day in any way we needed. We could never have done this without you.

NB—for every spreadsheet, every edit, and every conversation about how to build and run a business, I'm grateful for your precision, your patience, and your kindness. I'm proud to be your mom.

To my mother, Judy Bernard—it takes courage to step up with the checkbook and back a tiny, floundering business and we are forever grateful for the support you gave us when we were starting out. Of all the things you've given me in life, I'm most grateful for the four best siblings I could ever imagine. With each passing year my sisters, Jackie Barron, Mary Jo McNeily, and Meg Koett; and my brother, Joe Bernard; and their spouses, children, and grandchildren become more and more important to me.

John—how could I have imagined the joy you would bring to my life when Kate called and said she'd met someone special? The fact that you were a package deal with Jack and Hudson was pure magic and as for James and Charlie—nothing could have prepared me for the overwhelming love I'd feel for my grandsons. Somehow with all four boys you make it look easy.

Shell—I'd be lost without you.

Amanda—my life and my business would look very different without our Sunday calls. Our thirty-plus years of friendship remarkably feels like we're just getting started.

And to my Berger and Lightfoot families and all my friends in Australia—I hope to have more time to travel in the future and spend time with all of you.

Finally, to Steve and Shereen—life didn't turn out the way any of us thought it would but I'm proud to call you both friends and am grateful for all the support.

Love, Ann

TO MY MOM, BEST FRIEND, AND BUSINESS PARTNER—people always thought it was funny how much time we spent together but I wouldn't have had it any other way. Our wonderful home growing up is the reason I want to help others achieve the same thing, and that's all thanks to you.

John—we met right as I was starting this business and you've supported me every step of the way—from listening to me vent to ripping out dirty carpets, you were always by my side. You've been the best husband and father and I wouldn't be who I am today without you.

James and Charlie—my little maniacs. Thank you for always making me laugh. You've given my life purpose and I love you with all my heart.

Tich—thank you for always being there and covering for me with the kids when we couldn't get home. I appreciate everything you do.

Dad and Shereen—I'm sure this looked scary from the outside at times but you've supported me no matter what. Thanks for believing in me and always having my back.

Nick, my best mate—you've not only been a wonderful brother but an excellent friend. Your original vision for what Done & Done Home could be lit a fire under us and your amazing spreadsheets have kept us on track.

To the rest of my wonderful, blended and extended family—the Bergers, Bernards, Sturgills, and Bellows—thank you for all your support on this journey.

Jack and Hudson—you guys have been excited about this potential book for so long and now it's finally real! You've known me since the beginning of Done & Done Home and I hope that watching this business grow has let you know that anything is possible.

Jill—if I could choose one person to do this crazy co-parenting thing with it would be you.

I lucked out when I married into the Pawlowski family—you've been warm and welcoming from the beginning. And to my brother-in-law Paul, thanks for seeing something special in Done & Done Home all those years ago.

And to my friends who check in and don't mind that, for the most part, I've been MIA for a decade—it took everything I had to grow this business and you stuck with me anyway. I love you.

Love, Kate

IT WOULD BE IMPOSSIBLE FOR A COMPANY TO GROW and succeed the way Done & Done Home has without the dedication, support, and guidance of others.

We couldn't have done this without our team. Organizing isn't always pretty. It can be messy, dirty, emotionally draining work and you show up every day with smiles on your faces dedicated to helping our clients. To the original five—Macky, Megan, Lise, Louise, and Erin—thank you for sticking with us while we learned to grow this business. And to the newer team members—Jeanne, Gail, Stephanie, Judy, Meredith, and Sylvie—thanks for hopping on board. Lisa, Lauren, and Brittany—thank you for all your hard work helping us run the business. Meri, where would we be without you? You've believed in us from the moment you and Ann got on that call five years ago and we wouldn't be where we are today if you hadn't joined us. And to Meg, our brain trust—thank you for always picking up, turning our nonsense ideas into beautiful words, and being our biggest fan. Our dream was to build a business where moms could work and still have time for the important things in their lives without having to sacrifice one for the other and you all made that a reality.

To the patron saint of Done & Done Home, Judy Durham Smith—you brought us in to speak at Stribling the first month we were in business and everything took off from there. And to the original clients who are still in our lives, thank you for supporting us all these years—Jen, Steph, Mary Beth, Heath, Cheryl, Patricia, Maris, Sydney, Katherine, Diane, and Mary.

To Kieran McAndrew at Liffey Van Lines—thanks for always having our backs and giving our clients the best service in the world. You set the standard for cool under pressure.

To Lon Epstein at the Junkluggers—boy are we glad we had lunch with you all those years ago! Done & Done Home would be a mess if we didn't have the Junkluggers to help us clean up.

And because it's not all fun and games, thank you to our friend and accountant Mark Stone. You've taught us everything we know and stuck with us even when we're sure the numbers kept you up at night.

To Glenn Grant at Selfassembled Coaching—thank you for believing in us and teaching us how the big dogs do it. We didn't know we needed you until we met you and now we can't imagine growing this business without you.

To our amazing photographer, Julia D'Agostino—you're not only a joy to be with but an absolute professional. And thank you to Willy, Meri, Jen, Mary Beth, Meaghan, and Steve and Shereen for letting us shoot in your beautiful homes.

To our agent, Leigh Eisenman at Wolf Literary—thanks for hearing our call across the universe when we put our book idea on our vision board and you called the next day. You've been a wonderful guide through this process and we appreciate your brilliance, your humor, and your kindness.

To our team at Chronicle—Cara Bedick, Pamela Geismar, and Laura Mazer—thank you for letting us write the book we wanted to write and for making it so much better and more beautiful than we ever could have imagined.

Love,
Ann and Kate

Index

About the Authors

ANN LIGHTFOOT AND KATE PAWLOWSKI are the mother-daughter team behind the amazing home organizing and move management company Done & Done Home, which was launched in 2011.

Between their in-home organizing services and online course, they have helped thousands of clients dig themselves out of domestic disasters and are now sharing everything they've learned in the process.

Done & Done Home has been featured in dozens of publications, including the *New York Times*, *Domino*, *Architectural Digest*, *Good House-keeping*, *Real Simple*, CNN, *GQ*, *People*, and *Apartment Therapy*.

Kate holds a BA in psychology from the New School and is a graduate of The Nightingale-Bamford School.

Ann holds an MFA from the New School and a BA from Loyola University.

Ann and Kate live in a two-family home in Montclair, New Jersey.